ANCHOR BOOKS

HERE THERE AND EVERYWHERE

First published in Great Britain in 1993 by
ANCHOR BOOKS
1-2 Wainman Road, Woodston,
Peterborough, PE2 7BU

Foreword

Anchor Books is a small press, established in 1992, with the aim of promoting readable poetry to as wide an audience as possible.

We hope to establish an outlet for writers of poetry who may have struggled to see their work in print.

Following our request in the National Press, we were overwhelmed by the response. The poems presented here have been selected from many entries. Editing proved to be a difficult and daunting task and as the Editor, the final selection was mine.

The poems chosen represent a cross-section of styles and content. They have been sent from all over the country, written by young and old alike, united in the passion for writing poetry.

I trust this selection will delight and please the authors and all those who enjoy reading poetry.

Michelle Abbott
Editor

Contents

The Hill Pendle

Oh Thou Pendle, majestic shape,
In mantle white and winter's drape,
Patient wait for spring's release,
Of bursting bud and green relief.

Spring is sprung and summer's here,
Pendle beckons to far and near.
Leaf is full and flowers wild,
Tempting the hand of every child.

Sky is bright with day anew,
Pendle bathes in morning dew,
Birds will sing in sheer delight
Swooping, gliding in glorious flight.

Autumn's gold and bracken brown,
Pendle dons another gown,
Quietly, sitting in stirring breeze,
Gazing down on shedding trees.
People watch with fond affection,
As Pendle changes in winter's direction.

Holly green and bright red berry
Christmas time and all be merry,
New Year's at hand, not long to wait,
Beloved Pendle, majestic shape.

Fred Jackson

Lady in Black

'Twas a beautiful day,
for Lancashire.
The showers had gone,
now it was clear.

We walked around the graveyard,
a place of some fear.
With stones bearing marks,
of a death, date and year.

Then my Lady in black,
with her hand brushed a tear.
As she knelt at the graveside,
so she could be near.

She recalled the sad day,
when he fell from the pier.
And after she'd told him,
'To keep off the beer.'

Michael Robinson

Lancashire to Me

As a child I was told of Healy Dell
Shown the place where fairies dwell.
In bluebell wood played hours and hours,
Making dens, collecting flowers.

On Sundays we would all set out
To trek the moors and lark about,
Picking wimberries for the pies;
Make the most of lighter skies.

I never was a trotters fan,
I buy tripe, but just for gran.
Black puddings are to mother's taste
And winkles I have not yet faced.

The winding roads with passing places;
Fields of sheep and open spaces.
Fish and chips for Friday tea -
All this is Lancashire to me.

Suzan Wood

Home at Twilight

Be witness to each sparkling light
of Naples Bay at night-time
if you must;
but leave for me the views
each twilight time renews,
and have me feel content
with the sentimental
mood evoked by
brightening street and house lights,
in the misting, arcane valleys
of sprawling Pennine foothills,
as dusk's soft shadows shape
changing Lowry landscapes
of jumbled homes and tangled roads,
under a setting blood-red orb -
the very same,
that sets mill window panes aflame.
Let me breathe in deep
the heather-scented air
and listen to the sound
of moorland sheep
and night birds all around.
Not for me those Naples lights,
or the seven hills of Rome.
Let me gaze from craggy heights
at the magic of the night's
near-distant view,
and listen to
the quiet upland peace
of the place that I call home.

Denis Taylor

My Best Place

My place of birth -
a quiet place,
among the Surrey hills;
and then a place
in Lancashire
with its dark satanic mills.
And there I stayed
for forty years
amid the smoke and grime,
until I came
to my present home
a gentler, warmer clime.
Where I can walk
in broad, green fields
or watch a fox at play,
then sit and dream
of what might have been
at the closing of each day.
And know the peace
of the countryside,
warm sun and gentle rains,
and I will bide
where I love best,
mid the rolling Cheshire plains.

Eileen Taylor

Tar Covers Past

Tar covers past
where I live.
Today.
Intermingling of
events gone,
and those already ahead,
are there.
Words lost in accents,
Alive,
Old traditions are
reaching forward,
on my street.
We survive.
Accents cast aside,
We watch our lives
In the shadow
of the South.
We will live,
and reign.
And rain
shimmers
tar-covered
cobbles
where I live.
Today.

Fiona Barron

The Tidal Bore at Arnside Cumbria

A damp wind scours the great bay and the mist
Is lifting from the pier, there comes a hush
That falls upon the listening edge of land
And stills the talk of walkers on the sand.

The siren hoots its serious appeal
Come in! and soon the gradual waters steal,
Onto that shining temporary expanse
Which lay for hours between the sea and banks.

Quite suddenly, the currents, marshalling force
Advance a low white ridge within the course
Of Kent's bright channel. They foam then double back
Disperse and cross in planned eccentric track.

A reverent murmur stirs along the shore
Of admiration for this subtle bore
Whose work seems almost done. But there are still
Some higher reaches, corners left to fill
And ponds among the seagrass.

The waters lap and cover each in turn.
We have so much to do and always yearn
To flood a world of tidelands;
Estuaries, bays and coves
Await the ministrations of our love.
We'll make towards the west now, watching friends
For well we know our task can have no end
We're off past Walney Island, back to Mann
And Eire across the sea.

Stephen Hunter

The Beauty of Lancashire

Out of the window of the train
Looking out at the rain,
Such a dreary day
Yet the view took my breath away.

Such beauty all around
The landscape so serene,
Peace after the clatter of the day
The bustle of the town seemed so far away.

The hills in all their splendour
Calling out through time,
A faint mist rising
Enveloping, yet not quite hiding the beauty.

The meadows so alive and wet
The colour *oh* what lovely shades *God* as set
Hues of green, purple, yellow and red abound
This patchwork of colour I observed without a sound.

Quaint little cottages and farms as if asleep
Animals grazing, not a care not a peep
So peaceful so serene
Thank *God* for the country, with its humility.

M Threlfall

Cheshire

This county of contrasting scene
Brushed with varying shades of green,
Of houses grand, and cottages small,
Of grassy meadows and crags so tall.
Who knows what hidden treasures lie
Behind those Cheshire hedgerows high?
What gardens bloom for our delight
So fragrantly, just out of sight?
Cheshire! I love your country lanes,
Your market towns, your rolling plains.
We know that change must sometimes be,
But not too much for us to see.
Keep your charm, your beauty rare
For those of us who will always care.

Mary Walker

Blackpool Beach

. . . and the beach waits

baking in sun-heat,
feeling the feet
of many people.
Trippers skip
and run and laugh,
playing in a day full of sun.

. . . and the beach lies

now cool at evening,
trippers gone elsewhere.
There gulps the sand
at coins and rings,
forgotten sparkling things.

. . . and the beach feels

this new-found wealth,
starts to slide,
shelving under a silent tide
to count these riches
in secret.

John Fazackerley

Lancashire Dream

The night was cold, I could not sleep.
I wandered down the lonely street.
The only sound my ears to greet.
The echo of my walking feet.
Then all at once the street was changed,
with visions of a bygone age.
I saw it all, as in a book,
that someone held and turned each page.
The well lit street was now alive,
with visions I could scarcely see.
Where once I knew the Town Hall stood,
now in its place an old oak tree.
And yet again, a sight I knew,
the soldiers statue to heroes dead.
Now in its place a soldier stood,
a shining helmet on his head.
Stood by his side, no doubt his wife,
with bonnet cape and parasol.
A look of fear was on her face,
as if she heard the church bell toll.
I could not stand to see that look,
so turned around the other way.
Towards the once depressing houses,
which now looked lively bright and gay.
For now twas morn, the sun was shining,
people walked along the street.
Then men were walking to their labour,
all had clogs upon their feet.
The girls wore shawls, all looked weary,
eyes a staring straight ahead.
With pasty face and drooping bodies,
they looked more like the living dead.
Before I knew what I was doing,
I'd joined the crowd, walked up the hill.
We reached the top filed through the gate,
and now all walked on into the mill.

Inside I scarce believed my eyes,
filth and dust, dirt and grime.
With rows and rows of looms stretched out,
the only way to talk was mime.
Amongst the workers in the mill,
boys and girls not in their teens.
I stood there feeling quite disgusted
and waited for the changing scenes.
At last woke from out the dream,
to see at last the things I knew.
The motor cars and well dressed people,
buses, trains, to name a few.
Well lit mills and good conditions,
things that now we know so well.
Teenage children, not with clogs on,
wait at school to hear the bell.
Now when things aren't as they should be,
or if I'm bored the day seems long.
I think of days I could have lived in,
I feel like bursting into song.

Ernest Preston

My Beloved County

Your welcomed by satanic hills,
And of pastures green and pure.
There's nowhere else like Lancashire,
Of this I'm very sure.
From the mystic legends of Pendle,
To the busy bustling towns.
From bleak and beautiful Bowland,
Rare treasures can be found.
The Pennines form the eastern fringe,
Of a county full of features,
Providing natural habitats,
For a variety of creatures.
The concrete of the M6 river,
Meanders on its way,
Through the history of cotton,
Where the heart of commerce lay,
Canals which once brought life blood,
To factories by the score,
Now bring many tourists,
Who yearn for tranquil shores.
West we go to find the sea,
For frolics and some fun,
From Morecambe down to Southport,
You'll even find the sun,
If you've never been to our fair land,
Then these pleasures you have missed,
For when the Lord created Earth,
It was Lancashire that he kissed.

Margaret Derbyshire

St James' Churchyard in January

The buds are early in the North this year
and they catch in my mouth as I pass at dusk.
Gravestones are scattered everywhere,
like visiting cards left by the dead:
sunk like manholes covering drains,
buttressing transepts short of repair
with good three-inch granite.

Muscular memories etch with a flourish -
the Moseleys (of Moseley Street) the Birleys
and Broomes - planted in topography, their epitaph
a city's grimy, peeling, slave-scarred halls.
Competition's here, its monuments bristling,
as liveried Cotton shoves Wool to wall,
smudged soot-black into sandstone pink
as guinea-pigs, where thick brass plates
tarnish titles and old faded names
like *Hallam, Jemima, Japhet* and *Grace*.

Raised over plague-pit, in this hilltop fortress
with sheer drop to the river over Fletcher Moss,
I see no urns, no flowers, no burials,
only shadows under trees which gawp at bones.
At the lych-gate there's a sense of being watched,
in their boxed enclosure with rusting roof,
where nothing goes through, neither way,
that's not been paid for.

Alison Guinane

A Portrait of Northern Life

Smoke from factory chimneys hung around a sooty sky,
Images of matchstick people spewed from pits nearby.
It's taken years to rid the North of Orwell's morbid scenes:
The road t'pier and clogs and shawls, and ragged clothes on bairns.

What once was Wigan Borough is Metropolitan . . .
where girls no longer scrub the floors, for woman equals man.
Some women work while men stay home - no longer *woman's place*.
Anyone's a breadwinner in the North. I rest my case!

Tops and whips, and skipping ropes were games of long ago.
Our kids don't go t'pictures now . . . they watch a movie show.
They mega drive and rap and rave, not ballroom - more disco.
Flat caps for rain, and rarely seen, it's baseball caps on show.

The cotton towns that Lowry sketched are kept in Heritage.
The weaving looms, canal boat rides are there for every age.
Town centres portray Galleries of crystal, clothes and glitz:
We don't wear browns and coal-dust grey; it's a trendy shoppers' blitz.

We eat lasagne not clog-iron soup, in wine bars and restaurants.
But fish and chips and Lancashire Hot Pot's still there for the want.
The trams have gone from Wigan, but at Manchester and Blackpool,
They rock and rumble down the tracks, to work, and play, and school.

Then there's Wigan's rugby giants - the conquerors of Wembley:
A team of sporting heroes whom all the others envy.
The bid for Olympic status is now a northern aim.
Who would have thought in smoky chimney days
We may host the Olympic Games?

The buildings of the North have changed, the smoke has blown
away.
New towns now stand on fields of corn, a few remain to stay.
The wildlife parks and country manors pushed slag heaps
underground.
We can sail the coast or fly abroad . . . Northern freedom has been
found.

Those images of long ago now hang on museum walls:
Few cobbled streets, more motorways, ring roads and shopping
malls.
The markets, shops and houses huddle round church and steeple,
And inside you'll find the warmth they hide,
Pride of the Northern people.

Audrey Fairclough

Chester

I close my eyes, and what do I see?
a city of beauty,
. . . fantasy.
The walls of eternity, we're safe and sound
no violence found
around.
The park and the river in the summer sun
having fun
everyone.
Buskers at the cross, some alone, some in a pair
music floating in the air
everywhere.
Some are true, but some are lies
the solution for the words we despise?
. . . fantasise.
Homelessness and crime, hand in hand
drugs across the land
not banned.
When I open my eyes, what do I see?
a city of mystery
. . . reality.

Rebecca Dewnehy

Cheshire's Disappearing Landscape

England's green and pleasant land,
In between the cities of the North,
Cheshire was once a beautiful place,
Until developers shouted *'come forth.'*.

Then city folk all left in droves,
In order to make a fresh start,
Arriving in Cheshire via buses and rail,
Where once travelled horses and cart.

New towns have pushed the countryside East,
As the need for new housing goes on,
The ever increasing rate of divorce,
Means two houses are needed not one.

The sun has to rise behind high rise blocks,
Leaving the grass to dry on its own,
And the birds search in vain for the early worm,
But the soil has been covered by stone.

But as time goes by the cities and towns,
Now deserted and left all forlorn,
May become a green and pleasant land,
As the landscape is reborn.

In cities and towns like Liverpool,
Where the grass now grows green and firm,
And the birds will fly West from Cheshire and beyond,
In order to find their worm.

Then developers will turn to the cities again,
To give them a brand new face,
With city folk returning, giving Cheshire the chance,
To again be a beautiful place.

Paul Shelbourne

Overview

From here, I can see distant ships,
Migrating specks on a blueing sea sky.
Hedgerowed green tumbles and ambles away,
To where the grey spray swirls and spits,
Rolling and falling on shingle heard talking
And softly on sand, whose silence is golden.

From here I breathe air, sharp, bright and keen,
Diamond-clear birdsong calls: wind carry me.
The hill sheep preach loudly: bare into strong breezes,
From lowlands echo answers: be grateful for thick fleeces.
High trees huddling lean and whisper; wait for us, above,
White clouds waver and press on to the sea.

At night the sprawl-town flickers and beckons,
But, far away, the lighthouse winks its coercion.
With growing intent, it winks again,
Showing the cool knowing of an old night-watch
Who holds sea and land alike in his warming, warning, turning gaze.
The old night-watch, sees light in the darkness,
And keeps night's secret unspoken.

Christopher Lawson

The Artist and the Southdowns

May I look: O, yes!
That is very nice:
Orange sun in misty sky
paints such a peaceful picture.
I like the way the tufts of grass
pick up the glow,
and how you've caught the mystery
of those distant Downs.
That naked tree's a moving touch
- it brushes naked me.
You really are a skilful artist,
so well conceived, deftly executed,
brilliantly sustained:
        Congratulations Son!

Graham Claydon

The River Medway

The Medway in its muddy garb,
Awaits the freshening Spring.
Brown, like a sliding snake,
It sheds the many skins of winter.

Shaking gold, the catkins hang
In copse and river bank.
Starred in white, the garlic blooms
With celandine and violet.

Trumpets of wild daffodils,
Call on a winnowing wind
To winter, hunchbacked, moving slow,
The swollen Medway flows.

Margaret Gibian

Rochester -Upon - Medway

The living land is at my door
and I could never wish for more.
Trees of apples, pears and cherries,
logan, tay, and raspberries.
Luscious strawberries, by the ton -
they were picked for Wimbledon!
Or I can drive, then stop the car -
I'm glad this viewpoint's not too far -
And yonder gaze, when at my leisure,
for it gives me so much pleasure.
Beneath the bridge the Medway goes,
with twists and turns it gently flows.
Towards the sea, past castles bold
that did invading forces hold:
At Rochester and Upnor seen -
such tales are told of what has been!
Ancient Cathedral, standing there,
eight hundred years of wear and tear
have not marred your noble line,
from crypt to soaring spire, you shine.
My eyes can follow the High Street,
where Dickens' lovers find a treat
At Eastgate House where they can look
at animated scene from Book.
At Restoration House, it's said,
that Charles II went to bed,
And Henry Eight was often seen,
to Dover bound - another Queen?
The shops invite you to look around -
their range of goods is quite profound:
Ceramics, flowers or teddy bears,
or paintings, crafts and antique chairs!
Moored on the river, yachts in line,
a craft afloat where you can dine.
And if I glance towards my right,
a sight of engineering might.

The bridge for M2 motorway,
its graceful lines quite a display.
Now on my left is Chatham Town,
its Dock Yard once had world renown,
From Nelson's ships all made of wood,
to modern navy, all were good.
And 'tho its closure caused much strife,
it's slowly coming back to life;
A live museum of our past -
a shipping heritage, to last.
Commercial shipping chugs its way
along the river every day,
Past modern buildings on Estate,
the pace of life does not abate.
You see now why I love to look,
at this, my living History Book.

Grace Smith

Come to the Willow

Come to the willow
down by the stream
and dream with me.

A gentle breeze is rustling the leaves,
The sun is filtering through.
A dragonfly skims by on shimmering wings
And it's gone.
Come to the willow
down by the stream
and dream with me.

Two blue butterflies like tiny fragments of the skies,
Are dancing together on the breeze,
Not a care have they but to live for a day
In the sun.
Come to the willow
down by the stream
and dream with me.

A blackbird sings as it closes its wings
And settles on a branch of the willow,
It's pure notes cascade as we rest in the shade
Far below.
Come to the willow
down by the stream
and dream with me.

Sheila Brain

Beautiful Surrey

O'er twenty years I've viewed the county
and tasted the fruits of Surrey's bounty,
from home-grown food to world-wide fayre
delicious variety all are there.

In marketplace and roadside stall
there's fruit in plenty for one and all,
to corner shop or supermarket
I take the car, oh where to part it?

Give me the freedom of the country road
the wheels that take me from fixed abode,
to feast my eyes on season's colour
and observe the change whate'er the weather.

Let me scan the length and breadth
and soak up all that nature giv'th,
observe the growth and animals too
and raise my eyes to skies anew.

A creative force that knows our need
for tranquil fields of full blown seeds,
wheat and mustard, apple and grape
they're harvested before too late.

I think of the farmer and labourer too
and realise the work they have to do,
all is so ordered and neatly kept
as if all's done before they slept.

Country cottages with roses and thatch
public houses where doors have a latch,
winding lanes where cars take the strain
then turn the corner and feast yet again.

Lorna May Noah

Surrey Scenes

The tree clad hills and winding lanes,
The village inns, and church top vanes,
Remote farmhouses, old hedgerows,
The cottages where roses grow.
Commuters pass them every day,
As in a rush they speed away
To London and the endless grind,
Surrey's quiet charm is left behind.
And when they reach the end of day,
Tired workers make their homeward way,
Past manors, parks and cricket greens,
And ducks that paddle shallow streams.
Commuterland, to some, maybe,
To others peace, tranquillity,
With wooded glades and rambling downs,
Surrey's beauty wears many crowns.

Isobel MacCallum

Whitstable

The heritage town of Whitstable is famous for its oysters,
With oldie-worldie shops around, but no cathedral cloisters.
The oystersmacks have big bright sails with lobster pots aboard,
Oysters are sold in restaurants at prices you can afford.
Some ancient yawls have been restored and used here day by day.
An oyster or two is good for the bones or so traditionalists say.
The museum shows how life used to be with stunning lifelike
displays,
For a glimpse of Kentish history, on Whitstable feast your gaze.

Alison Kinnaird (11)

Springtime in Kent

You waited for me in your car,
To start our walk, though not too far.
We chose a route shown on a card,
Our first one, so not very hard.
Lovely you, pink jumper, blue jeans,
Always the answer to my dreams.

From Tudeley church to fields and stiles,
We ambled slowly o'er the miles.
Walked through Bank Farm, a pretty sight,
With baby lambs for our delight.
Bluebells, primroses, wild flowers,
Places we could stay for hours.

The birds were singing in the trees,
We also heard the humming bees.
It was so peaceful everywhere,
So we took time to stand and stare.
Through the fields to Capel churchyard,
The walk so far had not been hard.

The sun it shone for us above,
And all could see we were in love.
We got lost several times that day,
And twice we had to ask the way.
Bouncers Bank, Rose Cottage, we found,
Then a rabbit, we saw it bound.

On through more fields and woods we went,
Round in a circle our intent.
It all went well, the church in sight,
Back to Tudeley, we'd got it right.
These memories will linger on,
And fill my thoughts now you have gone.

Denis Terry

A View of Bexhill

Atop its hill, the sea in sight,
Timbered houses, dressed in white.
Few folk around, a sleepy air,
Has this place of life a share?
Manor House gone, the forge no more
And Belle Hill severed to the core.
Stands the old clock at ten-to-five
Is this village still alive?

Chantry Lane, a narrow green tunnel
Cars to and fro as through a funnel
Does this place possess a heart?
No dress shops, bank or supermart?
Just post office, pharmacy, general store
Newspapers and sweets, antiques galore.
Stands the old clock at ten-to-five
Is the village still alive?

Troops of Hanover marched through here
And village maidens held them dear.
Billeted they were in Barrack Hall
Shortly before Napoleon's fall.
Military gone, all quiet again:
Trees gently drip in sea-softened rain.
Stands the old clock at ten-to-five;
Is the village still alive?

Manor Gardens, an apron of green,
With stone-clad walks, the ruins between.
St Peter's Church, Lychgates and Linkwell,
All for the visitor long tales to tell.
Fine Barrack Field in which children play
New Church Halls where all have their say
Stands the old clock at ten-to-five:
Yes, this village is alive!

Shirley Read

A Deserted Castle in Rye

Bored and burdenless; he strolls towards the castle;
A scaffolding straddled block on the landscape.
Miles over the fields he treads, sheep stretch far;
As does their pelleted waste (This is gingerly avoided.)
Sun has killed the clouds and fries the unprotected land,
(And him) but progress makes the fortress loom.

Inside; not a soul but he inside; No-one to avoid.
It's nice, being empty, but builders' waste throughout the yard,
And fresh fag ends betray some recent visitor. Perhaps *he* left
That crumpled bag of KP Skips inside the Tudor rose;
Incongruous flash of now inside a glimpse of then.
(The lapis sky is framed by glaring walls
Blinded and bleached by incandescent sun.)
Sweating, he mourns his car-bound camera.
He'd like to capture this place, this scene, but can't,
And irritation drives him out the castle door.

Later, having left and walked away, he turned,
Looked back, and couldn't help but think again.
It looked smaller than it was, different and strange;
An awkward lump on a dead straight line;
Caught between land and air . . . he shrugged.
(A timeless intensity; Man vs Universe; eternity distilled . . .)
Feeling odd, he turned again; pondered anew;
'Poetry's impurity; debased depiction of truth.'
'It's not the same as being there' he said out loud,
And thought no more.

Larkin would have laughed.
It's funny what a bit of sun and solitude
Can do to the wandering mind.

J A Bowe

Sweet Memories of Sussex

Stationed there during the war
I loved the countryside I saw,
The winding lanes so very graphic
Picturesque with little traffic.

Barrage b'loons beneath the sky
Kept the *doodles* flying high,
A few were hit by British *Fighters,*
But others dropped - the rotten blighters.

Less pollution by the cars
No lights, so one could view the stars,
Gleeful biking along the roads
Watching squirrels, birds and toads.

That lovely ride down to a wood
But oh - the agony I stood,
Returning up an endless hill
Puffing so, I felt quite ill.

It therefore gives me greatest pleasure
More than I could ever measure,
That we've returned to Sussex borders
Minus flak *and* Army *orders.*

K M Blackwood

Beside the Road

The day began like all the rest,
Walk the dog, wash and dress.
Start the car, off to work,
Unaware of events about to lurk.

The usual heavy morning traffic,
Acknowledgements from passers-by.
Simple decisions, comfortably made,
From the car's warm electrically operated interior.

And then, there he was,
Something different to be seen.
Is he carrying shears?
Is his bicycle green?

An elderly countryman,
Motionless by the road-side.
Quiet amidst the bustling morning,
But shouting loudly of our times.

What will he do with his shears?
(There are no gardens near.)
Was his bicycle stolen?
(So much of that about, we hear.)

Forty years ago his purpose would be plain,
And he would stand one of many.
This morning, amidst the morning rush and trance,
His presence seemed an irrelevance.

G W Tarrant

Home in Kent

Now I am back in England from lands across the sea,
with many memories of things that I have seen.
The burning sands of Middle Eastern lands,
where Bedouins with camels do ever roam,
the snow and crystal clear rivers and streams
of Europe's middle lands.
Whose history in many books are bound for all to read.

But for all these wondrous sights, to wander in this
green land of beloved Kent, with rolling downs and leafy
lanes, rich fields with Oast-House and small stone walled
churches standing by. Woodlands where birds do ever sing
in Summer time, this is the place to be.
For the towns, village and ancient city of this fair land,
have a rich history that spreads more than a thousand years.

Romans found the oyster here, Vikings rowed their boats to
here, passing great white cliffs that guard this land so fair.
Spring, Summer, and Winter snow that blows across our down
lands, to the sea where fine clipper ships once sheltered
from the winter storms, so long ago.
Kent a land of fine regiments of horse and foot that fought
in many a far land, men of this green and pleasant land.

Now as I wander around this fair land of Kent, and watch
the sun set low in the West, with many colours painters
on canvas try to catch.
To walk by the Medway, where once steam packet boats of day
trippers, sailed a short golden sea to the golden sand of Margate.
A river where Dutch fighting ships once fought, a river where a
man called Dickens, would often sit and think, with red sailed
sailing barges always running with a fair wind to set the river
scene. I am no Dickens, but I am glad I was born in our fair Kent.

Fred Gambrill

Glorious Goodwood

August arrives,
Time for the races,
Big, bright hats,
and anxious young faces.

The sun shines down,
On the racecourse,
Gamblers in the paddock,
Choosing their horse.

The Jockey's ride down,
To take their place,
Each and every one,
Praying they'll win the race.

The gates go up,
Away they go,
The Jockey's stand up,
Heads held low.

Round the bend,
And up the straight,
One furlong to go,
The spectators can't wait.

They go past the stand,
Everyone shouts for their horse,
They cross the line,
They've finished the course.

Whether you're richer or poorer,
At the end of the day,
Everyone will enjoy,
The outstanding firework display.

Lyndsay Perry

Summer in Sussex

In the full sun's strength
We walked together,
The palpable heat
A blanket for our stride.
Those buzzing, darting flies
With rapid wing beat
Tried to tap our bodies
Even in the shade.
Our cries swung upward
When we sighted the freed
Profusions of foxgloves,
Leaning bell towers
Of the tree-felled glade.
With lilac-coloured orchids,
We kept watch, guarding
The seeded precincts
Of the grassy sward.
We were amused
Amidst maunching bullocks,
Tails flapping, as they haunched
Us further down the field.
We viewed the distance
And saw bright sunlight
Yield and soften into
An azure haze of blue.
All this for our pleasure,
Leisured companions
Of a summer afternoon.

Pat Howell

The Royal County of Berkshire

Early in the morning, a soft haze covers the Royal Berkshire Downs,
Weak sun beams trying to filter through the mist,
A noise like thunder disturbs the golden silence, the earth pounds,
Drumming horses hoofs, and the sport of Kings appears,
Muscles tense, sweating, racing into the distance leaving echoing
sounds,
Church bells ring over little Hamlets, homely cherished ways,
Many various crafts, carried on through the age,
The smell of burning, spiralling smoke from thatched cottage
gardens,
In the Spring, flowers and fruit grown in abundance,
In Winter like dormice beneath a blanket of snow villages go, cold
days,
Lazy Summer, hanging baskets bloom, coloured butterflies,
and busy bees,
Basingstoke, Reading Maidenhead towns and more, building our
future, our dreams,
Leisure centres, parks; football fields, cricket, golf and bowling
greens,
The river Kennet silently wends its way, the canals
reeds in harmony gently sway,
Elegant boats cruise along beside brightly coloured barges,
Past stately homes, through busy towns of shops, schools,
universities each day,
Inns, hotels lawns sweep down to its edge, fishing and
picnics by the river side,
Summer Fetes, race courses, regattas all, then in
the winter the Kennet is an ice rink,
Newbury home of the computer, and Aldermaston, exploring,
searching knew ideas,
Amidst the old there are new beginnings, of highways the
Counties Cities link,
Leading to the South, to England's heartbeat London City,
Continuing to the North, East, West, trains carrying freight,
motorways being built,

Nations flags flying high above administrative buildings,
a shared future, exciting,
Past farms and cows, sheep, fields of crops of hope stretching miles,
Windsor Castle stands aloof, cold grey brick, as if on another planet,
This County that has earned its name Royal,
As you bask in your glory, guarding our heritage, steady as granite,
England's Royal Berkshire my bounty, my home, my County.

M Bowers

Danebury Ring

Now the sun
Shines bright above,
Magical Danebury Ring
Ancient wisdom whispers
As the birds begin to sing.

Before the very coming
Of that greatest star,
People dwelt within this wall
Worshipping the universe
The sun, its rise and fall.

So close to mother earth
In her womb the Celts did live,
Feeling safe from brother man
But when sieged did not forgive.

Empowered by death and mystery
Bones kept, whilst flesh decayed,
For this was their sacred place
At whose centre many prayed.

In the moonlight, stones were slung
Grain was stored in mud and dung,
Wooden armour to the fore
Weapons forged from iron ore.

Ornaments of bronze were found
Multiple graves in shallow ground,
Memories of hard work and strife
A microcosm of Celtic life.

For Danebury Ring stands high on hill
A visionary glimpse as man stands still,
An Iron Age capsule, fallen from grace
Many enchanted by this place.

For where mystique in this hill-fort reigned
A canopy of trees, its life force feigned,
For no one knows, though history's akin
Still Danebury Ring holds its secret within.

Bruce Challis

Blake's Lock

Did you know
ghostly barges
slink past Blake's Lock
in the deepest part
of the night?

Carrying their cargoes
of biscuits
and malt grain
to Victorian ancestors,
who grow fatter
and drunker,
in their woebegotten Wharves
edging the Kennet.

As dawn breaks
they fade away,
leaving the towpath
to the rapist,
and the yuppies
and the cyclist
dodging the potholes.

Eileen Spencer Trott

A Wee Vale

'Tis a wee vale resting 'neath a hill,
Wi' a river running through,
Weear mill chimney standing straight and tall,
Guards t'old houses and the new.

Theear-sheep we gets wool from,
Run like mad across the moor,
And the auld folks has a smile and nod,
As ah passes by the doors.

We have a Glen, Wi' tram an all,
And folk come from afar,
To ride on't tram, to sit on't rocks,
Wi' sandwich and a jar.

We've cricket pitch in Roberts Park,
An football o'er river,
Then boats come art on Sundays,
Full on Mums and Dads wi' children.

Theears mi sister an mi brother,
Making tae, al day long,
Just in case a body drops on by,
An ah does - oft an on.

So all in all ah think its great,
Tho' some may not agree,
Yon wee vale resting 'neath the hills,
Is home sweet home to me.

Irene Glover

Lovely Lancashire

Lancashire lovely, so dear to me.
Lush countryside, rolling down to the sea.
Cobbles and cottages, villages small.
Towns of old splendour, cathedrals so tall.
Beautiful scenery, here at a glance.
Purple-grey hills in the distance, enhance.
Friendliest people are at your command.
To give you a welcome and kind helping hand.
The old country humour is second to none.
Always remembered when once you've moved on.
Museums and monuments. Church, folklore.
The heart of our England, here at the door.
Whether it's spring, summer, winter or fall,
Lancashire lovely will welcome you all.
Talking of Lancashire think of this scene.
A place to return to, when once you have been.

Joy Phillips

Sweet Wingfield

Oh sweet Wingfield, with its banks and streams
Where as a youth, I could sit and dream.
The sloping hill, where the manor ruin stands
The parapets, reaching upwards like pleading hands,
To close one eyes and hear the battles roar
As in olden days that's gone before.
And now, as we lift our eyelids gently clear
We see peace, tranquillity no trace of fear,
Fear, as in those days long gone past
As at the manor, where the Scots Queen was held so fast.
The village school, where youth so quickly fled
Where sometimes, by the ear a parent led,
A squalling infant, their pride and joy
But to the teacher, just another naughty boy.
Then how things changed as time went by
The tears that fell, as to teacher we said goodbye,
The stream, the woods, the birds that sing
Of you alone, just give me one small part
To lay my body, and rest my silent heart.

George Clark

The Street

At first, in loneliness, I switched it on,
And winding its way through my watching time
The Street became my waiting family.

It has warmed my heart and made me sad,
But like a glove in winter, it has comforted,
And given courage with its robust spirit and sharp wit,
Completely unawares.

Through weaving doorways it reveals, the mean, the good,
Old wounds and angry lurking sorrows,
And all the common needs of love are held within its frame,
A measured view of how we are, caught in a
Rainbow coloured span, a light for just a little while,
The Street lingers in the mind and in its way
Portrays us all.

C Lingfield

This World

This world could be a better place,
If we slowed down the pace
and looked each other in the face.
Everyone has feelings,
Life has meaning.
For those who have neither,
The experts have their healing,
be it, doctors or medicine or law.
We can correct what is wrong.
Why don't we stand up for the rights,
the right to correct our World.

Diane Hambrook

What Will Change the World?

What will change the world?
The sun, volcanoes and the sea,
Sorrow, sight, joy and peace,
This is why I'm me.

I want to see world business
Wearing a different suit,
And a new hat and coat to boot.
I want the children to have something
To look forward to,
The building of their lives
Is up to you.

If you're sitting there
A little confused by it all,
You're not on a different world,
Don't worry, stand tall.
There's so many of us
Who don't like the way it's all going.
But so few have the power
And they're doing it all wrong.

Thinking of their lives
Inside a bubble,
Wishing they were you.
And at the first sign of trouble,
You've got enough saved,
So you can shoot through.

If it all goes down,
You won't feel it like us.
You wouldn't even care
About all of this fuss.

Gordon Allen

No Common Ground

The churches are largely ignored
the young roam around bored,
for idle hands, there is nothing to do
with bricks, windows are put through.
The zest of life died long ago
only unhappy faces are now on show,
skies always appear misty and grey
trouble simmers more and more each day.
The warmth of Lancashire has disappeared
in its place, misery has been steered,
by a Government who created the North/South divide
and by their job losses, about which many hearts have cried.
Towns have become dirty and sad
they can't be bothered to fight for what they once had,
for they know that were they to get it back one day
again the Tories would come and snatch it away.
Prosperity cannot survive in the North
when John Major's trampling army steps forth.
So, in future, only votes by those classed as cranks,
will be given to the Tories in Lancs.

Graeme Doherty

Mersey Sonnet

Timid, her swell laps gently, so gently
We drift as one like mists of mellow night
Beneath her calm, the prowl of hidden might
She lifts, she falls as I watch intently.
Once caught, lights jig on her smooth rhythmic tide
But has she no bite, no sting resurgent?
So meekly she sprawls, this slumb'ring serpent
And I, forever watching, by her side.
How the restless seagulls thresh, how they shriek!
They rouse the pensive, they torment the weak
But stir as they do, shall never impose
I'm rapt by this temptress and her repose.
Now in her cradling, all joys unleashed
Home is the bosom of this tender beast.

David Ray

A Scene From Fleetwood Promenade

Old King Sol, the mysteries you revealed this night,
A scene a silhouette, I haven't seen for long,
For you, with all your power and might,
Can't permeate our clouded throng.

The grey and heavy vapours drown your rays,
And starved us mortals in this latitude,
But tonight you left me in a daze,
And proved your powerful aptitude.

You penetrated deep and far below,
Beyond horizon's depth your rays entwined,
The cragged Lakeland Hills, and valleys low,
What detailed visage ever so designed.

Astir with nature, as I ambled on my way,
Impressed by a view, no skill of man,
Or artist, with his brush could ever lay,
With every subtle colour could he plan.

The sky ablaze with hue, a vivid scene,
Intense, and brilliant, - I may be colour blind,
To describe that picture must be ever seen,
Detailed the landscape, perfectly defined.

Suspended there, between the sea and sky,
Remote and distant from our mainland shore,
T'was Mona's Isle, her Snaefell rising high,
Dear Ellen Vannin linked with us once more.

But gradually, the scene began to fade and die,
The sinking sun vanished out of sight,
And darkness mingled with the starlit sky,
I lingered with my thoughts, into the night.

Beatrice Olga Bean

Untitled

Lovely Lancashire,
Land of light and laughter,
Place of trees and water,
Leafy lanes and rolling hills.
Gamboling sheep and gambling men,
Public houses and shopping centres.
Legends lost and battles won,
Fighting still!
The only place the *red rose* grows,
Lovely, lovely Lancashire.

C Dudley

Missing you all . . . Love Paul

When my big brother, went working away
Mum and Dad were as proud as could be,
Not abroad, just up Manchester way
But that seemed a long journey to me.

The move meant promotion, more pay
He'd be trained on a course to be boss
But he wrote in a letter one day,
He was homesick for Preston and lost.

So we'd wait for his visits at weekends
All anxious to see brother Paul,
Saturday night, he'd go out with his friends
And Sunday, be here with us all.

Now our Paul's not one to complain
But one weekend that he'd spent at home,
When at last it was time for his train
He told of the sadness he'd known.

'You don't have to go back,' said my mother.
'It's not right son, to be on your own,
Stay here with your sisters and brothers,
Where your safe and your loved, here at home.'

And he never did go back that night
Though he never lost sight of his goal
And twenty years on, he's a boss
Here in Preston, his hometown, our Paul.

Angela Mary Thompson

Valley of My Dreams

Tame valley, not a valley of lore
But we lived there, poor.
Twelve children we sat down to tea in shifts of four,
Our beloved mother had to scrub the floor.

Park Road, ran by our Tower Street House
And carried buses from Ashton onto Stalybridge,
Our home was built in stone
And in winter 'twas cold as a fridge.

Cotton Mills their smoke over our abode
And early morning brought men and women
Clattering past in clogs and shawls across the road,
They carried coloured hankies over dinner
They as Lowry's people, only thinner.

The war began and things looked bad
The local home guard enrolled by dad,
When searchlights danced across over sky
We lay in our cellar, damp and clammy
While the youngest of us cried out for mammy.

The days got bright, and Whitsun shone for us all
We walked for our Methodist Church and felt so tall,
On May Queen Day, Tame Valley was green
And our hearts were full when our sister was queen.

Time has gone by, Mum Dad rest in peace
We are still twelve, in number and none of us cease,
To think of our childhood it seems
Of our wonderful days together,
In the valley of our dreams.

Victor Shackleton

My Country

It's just a small island, divided in three,
England, Scotland and Wales, but we live peaceably.
It's history is envied by new, richer lands
Who try to define the respect it commands.

Its weather is frightful, its climate sublime,
Its customs unique and unaltered by time.
It's a Christian country, it's just and it's free,
Full of castles and churches - and afternoon tea.

It has the same problems as all countries do,
Crime, unemployment, pollution and flu.
Police are not armed but they enforce the law
With a stiff upper lip and a truncheon - that's all!

Its people prefer peace, but when forced to fight
Together, as one, will defend what is right.
They hold their heads high and bow down to no-one,
Their courage is famous and second to none.

South England is known for its beauty and charm,
God's fertile garden, peaceful and calm.
North England is known for its dirt and its grime,
Industry, hard work, poverty, crime.

To combat this imbalance, what did God do?
He made northern people his own *Chosen Few*.
He gave them fierce pride in themselves and their worth,
And warm hearts which made them *the salt of the earth*.

The lion and unicorn, St George and the rose,
All these things spell England, as everyone knows.
I was born in this country, so I understand,
Why there's nowhere on earth to compare to England.

Shirley Baxter

Halcyon Days (the Boys From the Callon in the 1930's)

Summer holidays, no more school, six long weeks of bliss.
No more tables, no more poems, these are the days I miss.

Hopscotch, cricket, top and whip, football and releevo
I'll draw a snake upon your back, my memories of long ago.

No Costa Brava, Tenerife, no even a trip to Blackpool,
who cares or bothers, no not I, as long as there's no school.

Sunburnt cobbles, sunburnt feet, tarmac bubbling in the street.
Beggars, vendors passing by, happy days, nice blue sky.

Off we'd go, down halfpenny brew, swimming trunks and towels,
no more boring ABC's no more boring vowels.

Then into Melling's Wood we'd dash, and climb a dozen trees,
rip our pants, tear our shirts, scar our bony knees.

Off back home, up halfpenny brew, all tired out and worn,
pinching apples on our way, it's good to be back home.

It's Sunday night in late August, all playing in the cool,
our Mothers shout, 'Come on boys, tomorrow it is school,' - 'Boo.'

The same boys from the Callon (in the 1940's)

Playing football, Waverley Park, it's nineteen-forty-three,
the captain shouts, 'Where's Tom and Dave,' they've both
gone off to sea!

Saturday night, off we'd go, and meet down at the pub,
talk about the penalty, we'd scored in all that mud.

When the landlord shouted 'Time,' we'd all go to the dance,
St Igs, Queen's Hall, Regent, whichever took our fance.

On our way home we'd grab a pie, Pickerings was the name,
the finest pies in Preston, renowned for all its fame.

As we staggered on our way, a little worse for drink,
we'd bang into the GI boys, enough to make you think.

The Yanks had lots of money, and a fair amount of Gum,
they'd stolen all our Women, to us it wasn't fun.

Well as the fight came to a close, and all received a bloody nose,
we all shook hands and went our way, we'd lived to see another day.
The same boys form the Callon (in the 1990's)

And now we're growing old and grey, we still all talk of yesterday,
the things we did, the fun we had, seems strange to
hear the word *Grandad*.
We sometimes meet our old friends, when we go up the Town,
But as you can imagine, some are not around,
Some have gone to live abroad, in far off foreign-lands,
and quite a few we'll never see, they died in enemy hands.

Austin Ford

An Ode to Old Ireland

I'd dearly love to take, a trip
Across the Irish sea
To take a look, at erin's isle
A dream come true for me.

I'd like to see, the shamrock green
A growing in a bound
I guess, I'd see, the little folk
A dancing, all around.

I'd see the little chapel
So very dear to all,
Also St Pat's Cathedral
Where he stood, in days of yore.

I'd take a walk, round Dublin town
Then sure, my heart would ache,
To go to Connemara
And sit beside the lake.

I'd also go to Doonerie
The wishing well, is there
I'm sure, I'd hear, Old Irish Tunes
A playing, in the air.

And when I'd had, a last long look
At this isle across the sea
I'd go, back home, to dream about
This Isle of Innesfree.

Gladys Harrison

Of Summers Gone

Where are the days when I was young, before I reached my prime?,
Even here in Wigan then, the seasons knew their time.
Summer seemed to guarantee a full six weeks of sun,
Tho' times were hard, and cash was short we all had time for fun.
Where are those summer days that blazed when I was just a boy?
We'd go for walks down country lanes;
Oh! life was such a joy.
In fields of grass that smelled so sweet, we'd while the day away.
Sky-larks twittered high above, and trees would gently sway.
The heavy scent of Hawthorn blossom filled the summer air,
As home we'd stroll at even-tide, we hadn't got a care.
People were so friendly then, the war had not long gone,
A peaceful feeling everywhere, the summers oh! So long.
Every door was left ajar, and on those sultry nights.
Groups would gather down the street, to sing into the night,
Everyone would take their turn, to sing, or say what's right,
In perfect harmony (it seemed), the tunes would fill the night.
Tired and drunk with happiness, we'd wander to our beds,
The mem'ries of the day just spent, still swimming in our heads.
Now; just recalling as I have, those days when I was young,
I can hear the songs, still smell the smells, that on those
summers hung.

Maurice Vizard

The Old Tod's Shining Bones

Fell sides smoked and pelted with bracken
Crimson in the colours of unmanned autumn,
Rust-like tints run wild too
Across heather hummocked broken boulder lands.

A wild and windward Westmorland day
Polishes the stones with a fear-reeking scent.
Dappled shapes that utter hound-dog cries
Flay and flog the tourist ravaged paths.

Beyond, beyond shrouded eyes survey a crackle boiling sky
While feet that once splashed a shrapnel of mud,
Now buckle and crumple to exhaustion's numbing smack
All is lost, a freedom shattered
Man silhouetted twists his binoculars with a simmering joy.

Pounce, pounce smiting jackal-like breath
Banshee music wailing an even more blood curdling note,
Jiggle, jerking fox tossed to the hound dog snap
Knashing, tugging shreds of pink; fanged embrace remorseless
Ten thousand questions dripping from a dry stone wall.

Mist sweeping off the crag tops in plumes
Like creamed back wispy hair from an old man's scalp,
Fissures and gullies, scars and scabs revealed
All those worry-lines troubled by the blood-lust
Of the hunt's stabbing, ripping, slavering glee.

Rain pouring off the crags in rills
The hard mountain now weeps for the fox,
Where men's eyes remained dry
The wind howls through the carcass bones
But the spirit's guile remains drifting, forever, drifting by.

Jimmy Eccles

The Tier of Tears

For some of us in the British Isles,
It's tea and crumpets, and lots of smiles.
For some of us in this blessed land,
It's croquet and caviar - isn't it grand?

For some of us in this Sceptred Nation,
It's briefcase and overcoat, from station to station.
For some of us under the Union Jack,
It's two weeks in Spain, and glad to be back.

For most of us in this Northern Shrine,
It's blood, sweat and tears, and the poverty line;
A cyclical motion, we can't win nor lose,
To eat or to heat - which would *you* choose?

Michael J Halstead

Childhood Memories of a West Riding Village Life - 1930's

Betty my friend lived at door number nine,
'Twas a cosy house, back to back.
Her father worked hard down a Yorkshire mine
Hewing coal, in the dark, dank black.

When each shift was done I saw men trudge by,
Their knee pads' slung low over head.
With faces coal black, their pink rimmed white eye
Made their mouths' glow a vivid red.

I never spoke, for I knew not who
Beneath all that grime there would be,
And always showed shock if a voice said, 'Ow do!
By gums lass, didn't tha know it were me?'

Yet I knew what time I must never knock,
Seeking friends with whom I could play.
When long slipper baths in each kitchen would block
The door, leaving no other way.

Grace Leeder-Jackson

A Trek Through Widnes Market

Within the covered market
Carpet cabins neighbour,
What could be Marks and Spencers knickers.
Take your pick
But look around,
Be struck by lack of luck
Cast a glance,
To where privilege is the front stage speck
To inspect the catalogue seconds
Track down a famous brand shampoo,
or the Clarke's real leather shoe.

Jayne McLaughlin

A Day at South Queensferry

The other day we all went to South Queensferry
The weather was great I got as red as a berry,
Kenny and Alfie went out in their boat
But they had to row to it first as it was afloat.
We took plenty of juice and lots of food
The kids enjoyed themselves which was good,
Lynda lay on the table and off came the blouse; oh what a glance
She said tell me when Alfie and Kenny are coming I said no chance.
Alfie took Lynda back to get a shot on the boat and said it wasn't bad
I held the kids on the rail to wave to their dad,
We drove to the cafe in the car

We could've walked as it wasn't far.
Back to the bench for another stay
By this time the men were far away,
The time came to go home we stopped our play
The sun was still shining what a glorious day.

Alison Swinton

Seaside in Winter

The seaside in winter,
The ships in the bay,
shelter from gales
'til a much calmer day.
The rocks on the seashore,
covered in foam.
The beach huts are locked.
The owners gone home.
The crests of the waves,
swirly and white,
on a grey Winter's day,
not a welcoming sight.
People all huddled
in bright anoraks,
wellington boots
and gabardine macks.
Warm woolly hats and
gloves on their hands,
striding along on the
ocean washed sands.
The rocks stand intrepid,
they've nothing to fear,
They'll still be standing
for many a year.
The seaside in winter
on a cold, crisp day.
Walk along quickly,
it's too cold to play.

Mavis Fox

Jericho Valley

Heron wild and willow watered
History heaves itself aloft
In the rise of ancient buildings,
Mines and heather covered croft.

Ancient stacks and tumbled workings
Now reclaimed by sea and time.
Softened by the hand of Nature,
Drifts of sea-pink, gorse and thyme.

Sun and wind and Cornish weather
All combine to claim their own.
Patiently restore, replacing
All the borrowed earth and stone.

Down the ancient coastward valley
Carving passage to the sea,
Man and Nature, turn and turn,
Have left their mark for all to see.

L M Turner

Our Day Out at the Beach

It's lovely to be here, free outside.
Walk the beach, dodge the tide.
Swooping seabirds, screech and shriek.
As carried fish, slip from the beak.
The roaring sound of seas, that shock.
As up on the land, it slams the rock.
Hissing foaming, showers high.
Marooned and stranded, starfish die.
With seaweed piled, up in a heap,
Brought in with the tide the mighty deep.
Driftwood lays around the sand.
As the might of the sea, brings it to land.
Darken footmarks made by me.
Erased in seconds by the sea.
On the horizon a smoking stack.
It must be our ferry, coming back.

W D Bowden

Progress

They've constructed a precinct where the trams used to rattle
Across Victoria Square like tanks into battle.
The once cobbled street with pavements natural stone flags
Has finally given way to machined concrete slabs.
At night, neon lights with impersonal glare
replace friendly gas lamps that once flickered there.
But the two couchant lions still stonily stare,
When will they be moved? if anyone dare.

Gone is the old open market with naphtha flare,
A car park and theatre are now standing there.
Redundant, removed, the old railway station
Old shops, quaint buildings and a conglomeration.
Of little side streets, straddled by the Town Hall
Are all gone and forgotten - at least hard to recall.
And on the music-hall site we knew as *The Grand*,
Vacant eyed office blocks usurpingly stand.

The tower on The Pike has fallen from grace,
To a modern TV mast it takes second place.
A reservoir has drowned what was known as The Jumbles,
A stream-riven valley where youth frolicked and tumbled.
Suburban encroachment has embroiled the surrounds
Where formerly farms, fields and pleasant haunts could be found,
New faces for old places, present takes over from past.
And those two Town Hall lions, how long will they last?

H Mossley

Cheshire

Cheshire is a county both green and fair
With winding lane and City square.
The finest countryside you have seen
Cricket matches on the village green.
Tourists walking Chester's famous walls.
The cathedral is an important port of call.
Rowing boats upon the Dee, canoe and paddle too,
Parties of young people out for a day at the Zoo.
Town Crier in costume, ringing his hand bell
Strawberry picking at farms, some in Kelsall.
Salt Museum, worth a visit, located in Northwich,
Narrow Boats negotiating one of many locks.
A train spotters paradise is the station at Crewe
(quickly cross the bridge, Inter City is due)
Delamere Forest with Nature Trail and walks.
Spread across the County are many Gardens and Parks
Old Farmhouses, hay stacks, fields of potato crops
Dairy herds on pasture green, Cheshire cheese is *tops*
Cathedral, Abbey, Manor House and grand Estates
Garden Parties, Strawberry Teas and Church fetes.
Tally ho! the riders call, starting off the Hunt
Jumping fences, riding hard, trying to be in front.
Horse Racing on the Rodee, the sport of men and Kings
Hallowed music in the Cathedral, when the choirs sing
Fishing on the Flashes and River Weaver too
Numerous sports halls, and leisure centres new
Berries in the Autumn and blossom in the Spring
The fragrance of many flowers summer time brings.
This is my County, the one I like best
Cheshire is the finest in the North-West.

Sheelagh Evans

The North West

Far from the south
Not in the east,
The North-West holds
The heart of the beast.

No pressing need to depend
On our other neighbours,
Our manufacturing firms
Supply what matters.

Our economy thrives
On what we export,
Our industry has lately
A lot to report.

We've much to boast
As far as our centres,
Airports, stations and shops
Olympic bid for starters.

Leisure and business
It's all here,
North-West must now be
The region of the year.

Lots to look forward to
Lots to look back on,
Surprising why we don't
Command all the attention.

Outstanding achievements
Are what we're about,
Proud as we may be
Medals we do without.

Warren Hughes

Returning to the Lake District

I had forgotten how
The mountains enfold you
In their strong arms.
How the clouds hang
Above the noble crags,
How many shades of green
In sinuous field are seen.
How rivers sing and sparkle
And lakes are bright then dim,
Where screes rush down
And trees hang over.
How silent paths from light
Lead through dappled woods,
Where trees so tall and straight
Hide the clouds from sight.
I had forgotten all this
But coming back again
I marvel at it all.

M P Denwood

Inertia

The fantasy of standing still in time
watching life fly by and changes take place.
But here lies the town who escaped her race,
tranquil she lay while refusing to rhyme.
Trapped by leaves, never reached the Winter line.
The iron rust of rides without a trace
of Spring or Summer, a town now laced
only with dying memories so kind.

The crowds with their flowery costumes ran
in search of something different, something cheap.
Blatantly useless, plastic toys saw man
look farther than where the sky meets the sea,
to more summered sites, and an attraction
far greater than that of Blackpool's beach.

Mel Machan

Our World

Ours is a world of sun and shade,
Where comedy and tragedy are equally played,
Where good and bad continually fight
In order to find the greater might.
Forces habitually kill sister and brother.
The sadness of it all shatters father and mother.
Uncertain joy and certain sorrow
Beg the question of the coming morrow.

Yet each coming year finds the poppy blooming amongst the corn.
Each day has a sun, thankfully, reborn.
Alas, our part is all too brief,
Our mortal lives ending in some grief.

How reassuring is the natural world
Dodging asteroids as it is hurled
Through space on its ordained course,
Smoothly gliding without a hint of force.
Yet grasp the nettle and it will sting.
Such simple truths eternally ring.

N Marshall

Liverpool Pride

So proudly she looks towards the sea,
Remembering, how it once used to be,
When she was paid homage by all the world,
Who sent their great ships, with flags unfurled,
The town was a hive of industry,
A bustling mass of energy,
An excitement buzzed throughout the air,
Which everybody seemed to share,
Whether folk were rich or very poor,
There was always an ever open door,
For that's how it was in old Liverpool,
A place where merchants used to rule,
Then one day they took their wares away
Leaving us all in disarray.
Quickly they went, like the outgoing tide,
Taking everything, but Liverpool Pride.
Now like the Phoenix, from the ashes she'll rise,
To begin a future, of enterprise,
Still looking proudly towards the sea,
As she writes a new chapter in History.

John Hurstfield

Westward

O're Hill and Dale in Somerset;
By luscious pastures, quiet rhines,
Through towns and cites
Full of interest and delight,
Walk through Cloisters, Cathedral Greens;
Pause awhile by Roman scenes.
Climb the Tor, and see the views,
Journey on to coastal bays:
Wooded cliffs and moorland ways.
Stags and Ponies roaming wild:
Country Inns of sheer delight,
To stay a while, or pass a night,
Onward, Westward, by coast or plain,
County town to Devon lanes'
Leafy roads, hedges high,
To explore as we draw nigh.
Cottages with Roses around the door,
Jasmine, Lavender, flowers galore,
Down to the Sea where the Yacht folk go,
Where the waters ebb and flow,
Race and sail these Coastal waters;
And revel in the Harbour Quarters.
Across the Bridge, we then shall go:
To Cornwall's Creeks, and open Moors,
Sandy strands and rocky pools.
At Land's End, our ramble o'er,
Now our steps must Homeward trek.
Call of the West, We will be back

Kay Fleming

I Remember Blackpool

My memory's fading, now let me see,
Yes, Blackpool, fifty years ago, 2100 AD.
A history lesson of our finest beach,
This is the sort of thing in school they should teach.
Gather round children, I'll tell you a tale
Of when Blackpool was first with the Hologram Rail,
It's commonplace now, but way back then
No-one had seen an invisible train.
And the Tower was shorter than it is now,
Only one hundred thousand metres or so.
The sand was still there then, but no-one sunbathed,
The air was still thick with the nuclear rays.
And Bingo was just a game, a craze,
Not an Olympic event like nowadays.
You see children it's always been the finest place
And now it's linked with America, that tunnel is great.
I'll take you next summer, if the weather's better than now,
Minus twenty degrees is a little too low.
We will see the latest robotic performance,
A full three ring circus on the ice-skating rink,
No children, it's not boring, Blackpool is great,
You'll be taking your grandchildren one day I bet!

Ruth Burgess

Yorkshire

There is a culture here
That combines qualities of yesteryear,
The intrinsic values that once were
Are being lost for reasons unsure .
With governmental decisions disbanding the cultures essence
The coalpits disappearing forever with the Prime Minister's blessing,
People that were once so strong and proud
Stand now with heads bowed.
These strong people were the only ones daring enough
To take on the Government and lose,
Showing courage and bravery with nothing else proved.
To live amongst these people is a lesson in life.
One that should be experienced by those in power
Before they make decisions that cause such strife,
To look for true men
Look for Yorkshire men.
For they are what
True grit is made of,
What a shame this is not
Recognised or appreciated by those above.

M Bensley

The Beautiful Haydon Valley of Wiltshire

I am looking O'er my Valley, it's
Five O'clock am
the Blackbirds, they are Chirping,
some Clucking, as they do.
City lights are in the distance,
so pretty, so silent, in their
lovely Hue.

Now, Dawn is gently breaking,
grey skies are overhead,
the Blackbird, he's still
singing,
seems he never goes to bed!

The City lights are going out,
replaced by Gods own Sunrise,
a glimpse of Heaven then appears,
just like a new sensation, of
happiness without Fears.

George Ponting

Greenham Common Song

December 1983 Voice inside said to me,
'You should go down to Greenham'
Rose at four and shut the door
On my sleeping children.
Ran apace in hot haste
To catch the coach to Greenham.
Snow slurried down but warm inside
Singing songs together.
Made a friend as we wend
Our way down to Greenham.

Fences high pierced the sky
But we circled round it.
Joined our hands it did feel grand
Singing round at Greenham.
Holly bright and Coppers' smiles
Hailed the Season's Glory
But soldiers' staves and orders grave
Told another story.

Felt a chill that boded ill
When they cut the Wire
Girls inside cried aloud
As armed men come to hound us.
Ran in fear as horses rear
Through the camps at Greenham.
Night came down and lights bobbed out
All around the common.
Sang our Song, can we be wrong
Wanting peace at Greenham?
Sang our song, can we be wrong
Wanting Peace for all men?

Avrille McCann

In Danbury Woods

(for Lora)

It was natural
To hold your hand in the woods
Far from your Cornish coast,
As we surfed the rustling swells
Of Danbury leaves.

You wanted to be carried,
To swing from my strength,
To be married with horseplay;
To be a girl on a cliff of love
Without fear of falling.

You dared me to throw you into the lake,
As if you wished to shatter
That silent mirror of water
With your body,
Absolve the past to flash
Wet as a new-born baby in sunlight.

My son, winging from the other hand,
Soared into the trees,
To return chirping
Winter word-clouds of wonder.
Your mother smiled -
We must have looked a family -

And for a moment your world was safe
Beneath the blue lake of the sky.

Frank Dullaghan

Yes We all Have a Place That is Special

Yes we all have a place that is *special*
Where delight and contentment abound,
A small glimpse of a gigantic pattern
Heightened by every sight and each sound.
There are brown ducks and white ducks and mallards,
Feathered flexible necks ringed in green,
They ride, proud, on the sparking water
Or rest by the edges and preen their sleek oily coats.

Like tiny beached boats,
Awaiting their next expedition.
If you throw them some crusts there's a flurry
To secure advantageous position,
From the far field an Army is marching
As the Canada Geese join the fray,
Swimming, skimming they glide on the surface
With a honk and a great spurt of spray.

Ever hungry for crumbs come the small birds,
Chirpy sparrows, then moorhens and coots
From the crevasses shaded by willows
In their sanctuary of the tree roots. When the limp winter's sun sheds it's pale glow
And the gulls have flown home from the sea,
Or in spring when the fledglings are hatching
Come, friends, and find beauty with me.

Alison Cox

Reflections

I sit alone on the cliff top, as I've often done before.
I watch the waves come rolling in, and break against the shore.
I feel a sense of tranquillity, as I survey the scene.
I close my eyes, I feel the breeze, is it really just a dream?

I walk slowly along the headland, no-one else in sight.
I turn my gaze to deep blue sky, a gull is in mid flight.
I see it soaring high above, and then it swoops down low.
I hear it's haunting echo, as along the cliffs I go.

I know I shouldn't linger, as the sky is turning black,
I want to capture every moment, before I head on back.
I button up my collar, as the wind blows round my head.
I cannot bear to leave this place, and go home to my bed.

I can see the light is fading fast, the storm clouds rush on in.
I turn once more towards the sea, the gulls they make a din.
I know they're trying to warn me, but I find it hard to go.
I now feel a sense of awe and wonder, it really thrills me so.

I hear the breakers crashing, down on the rocks below.
I stop to take just one more look at the ocean's mighty flow.
I walk a little faster now, as I head back along the track.
I try to ward off a shiver, as the rain soaks down my back.

I reach the tiny cottage, the tempest rages on,
I peer through the broken windows, not a sign of anyone.
I grasp the latch and give a push, the door creaks open wide.
I thankfully sit down to rest. I've found a place to hide.

I sit a while on the old stone floor, and ponder on its past.
I listen to the roaring sea, I'm sure the rain won't last.
I love walking on the cliff tops, in Summer sun or rain.
I know that come tomorrow, I'll be back here again!

Beryl Makin

To See or Not to See

I walked to work today
The same old streets, the same old way
People rushing here and there,
Hello! Good Morning! Do I care
Hurry, hurry, no time to spare.

Wait, that school, those children
Were they always there?
That dog with three legs, that girl with orange hair
Mrs Jones at 24, I've never noticed her before.

Market traders selling their goods
Stalls overflowing, flowers, fruit and black puds!
An Aladdin's Cave for any would be buyer
Look! a Hot Potato Man and even a Town Crier!

A hand reaches out, do I pass it by?
Do I stop? Not now, no time, no money, I lie
Inside I grieve, it could be me!
My hand reaches back, But I don't really see!

These streets, these people, and everything there
Are mine says God, take time, take care!
I love you, but I love them too
Oh Lord!, I cried, let me love them too!

With open heart he opened my eyes
He took my hand, made me realise
Thank you God for this new today
I see more clearly now, when I walk this way.

Kath Rigby

The Maid of Buttermere

(My yarning inspired his
about my humble sense of duty, my modesty, my beauty)

The fairest of them all, her charms must pall the cities
artifice, for painted mouths and rouged cheeks
no longer can entice the man who, tired
of London, seeks a freshness to his life.

Or pen, with which he phrased me a poet's muse,
or perfect wife. He praised my hair of brown, my eyes,
my lips vermilion red. He wrote of me, spoke not to me.
Not one word to me he said, but told his readers
Come and see the Beauty of the Valley, The Maid of Buttermere
The Landlord's lovely daughter, Sally!

So I erred, what's in a name, or face that
cannot be enhanced by brush or pen? I brought her fame.
Who'd know the wench, except my whimsy chanced
that day to find her fair, to write her fair.
With travel writer's flair to make them see as I had seen
and want to be where I had been.

So they came from far and near to view The Maid of Buttermere.

The writer found me serving, found my modesty unswerving.

Said he had done me wrong. In truth, his writer's skill
had promised beauty of my youth that time could not fulfil.
He had no doubt my shape, described as statuesque, soon
would be just stout! And thought it best to mention, gentlemen
of ill-intention, drawn by worded charm, to do fair Sally harm.

I thanked him for his kind concern and, not to be contrary,
but driven by his need of truth, said my name is Mary!
Then nothing's as it seems Sir, not this side of dreams Sir
For I believed in hope, and hope has let me down
Now they're hanging Hope this morning in Carlisle Town.

Catherine Klontz

No Green Outlook

As concrete city rises
Green belt - becomes obsolete,
Milling Humans - everywhere
Cars in every street.

What about our animals
Feathered friends as well,
Axeman cut down forest
Motorway - The Dell.

Hills and Moors are nearer
Campers - picnic too,
We hardly see a rabbit
No fawn - or crane in view.

We're only a small island
So keep what nature decreed,
Wild fowl and animal kingdom
For them a world that's freed.

Edna A M Cattermole

Thoughts on Leigh

I've travelled far and wide you see,
From Staffordshire to Anglesey,
Yet I return to Leigh.
From mountains high and valleys green
And Border towns where I have been,
Yet I return to Leigh
Worcestershire with country spires,
Malvern Hills and Severn shires.
Yet I return to Leigh.

As mills and factories close their gates,
Once carefree people paid their rates,
Now stripped of dignity.
Shops forced to close as prices drop,
Teenagers crowd in dens of pop,
Fathers push babies in their prams
Cross busy roads where once ran trams,
Or cast their lines on canal banks.
These men worthy of so much thanks,
Backbone of Britain's working might
Smile at a stranger and ask, *Alright*?

Elsie D Gee

Nature's Art

Seeing pictures in the sky
As the clouds go drifting by;
Human faces, animals too
Valleys, hills, one can wander thro' -
Wondrous scenes, that unfold,
What marvellous stories can be told!
The Hippopotamus grows in size,
Nature, exhibited before one's eyes;
Drifting at leisurely, stately rate,
Then slowly begins to evaporate.
Elsewhere in this silent scene,
Likeness of men who might have been
Here on Earth in bygone days;
Reappearing in a flimsy hazel
Expression changing, formed by the breeze,
Interpret it, it's there to please.
Lying at peace in the summer sun,
Plenty of time, the day not yet done;
The occasional hum of a passing bee,
Many more images yet to see.
The faint lowing from a distant field
Of a cow preparing its daily yield
Among others in the peaceful herd,
Their lowing as yet unheard
Until the time to give their milk
From udders, soft and warm like silk
How peaceful! I relax and sigh;
Then return to the gallery in the sky.

E Bocking

Look Up

Look up!
Cheer yourself up!
Look up at the sky and beyond!
Climb a high hill.
Take the trouble to go.
It's better than any big pill.

Look up!
Cheer yourself up!
Look up at the sky and beyond!
O travel up high,
With a freedom of mind
That even good money can't buy.

Look up!
Cheer yourself up!
Look up at the sky and beyond.
The clouds, pressing down
Hide a new universe
A mixture of known and unknown.

Look up!
Cheer yourself up!
Look up at the sky and beyond.
Beyond move the stars,
And the planets you know,
With lots that you don't, even Mars.

Look up!
Cheer yourself up!
Look up at the sky and beyond.
No confines of knowledge.
Imagine it all,
Spreading out, out and out, past the edge.

Look up!
Cheer yourself up!
Look up at the sky and beyond.
Swoop down like a bird.
See towns. See the sea.
And end when your vision is blurred.

Look up!
Cheer yourself up!
Look up at the sky and beyond.
The world appears changed.
It's friendly and kind.
No longer unkind and deranged.

Look up!
Cheer yourself up!
Look up at the sky and beyond.

Marj Norton

British Summer Time at All Hallows' Mitton

Walk a summer's lane to the church and its tower,
Reflect that the clock is forward one hour.
Enter by the gate and wait awhile,
Contemplate the centuries
Held captive in weathered stone,
Then tread the hallowed ground
To where the sundial stands, alone.
The sun has unfettered path across the sky;
In the gentle shadow there is no lie.
Watch closely to see that it will go
Where e'er the sun determines so.
When clouds veil the skies
The sundial fades and dies
In cooling shower.
Pillared stone becomes the grave of time
Yet time not dead,
For sunbeams wait to move again
The shadowed hour.
Leave with the gift of hope
That departed souls released from clockwork time
Share now the truth
Of the sundial's hour sublime.

Kenneth Tompkins

Howm A' Doin'

Howm a' doin' sit down flower
This will only take an hour.

Howm a' doin' - mustn't grumble
Can you hear my stomach rumble?
Got this pain that comes and goes
Don't tread on my hammer toes!

Howm a' doin' - not so bad
If you don't count the ills I've had
A wheezing chest, a cough that's rough
They've started making butter tough.

Howm a' doin' - doin' well
Is it just my feet that smell?
Did I tell you how I creak
Doubt if I'll be here next week.
My eyes are bad it's hard to see
Got to go I need a . . .

Come in doctor, ee I'm glad
Howm' a' doin' - feeling bad
What do you mean there's nothing wrong
Seen the colour of my tongue.

Doctors go from worse to bad
That's the fifth this year I've had.
Wrong! - I mean from bad to worse
Hello love - are you the nurse.
It's a blessing that you've come
I'm having trouble with me bum.

I hear them ask the wife 'How is he?'
But she never says that I've been dizzy.
She never tells how sick I've been
Or how my ears are turning green.

Won't tell of weeks I've spent in bed
With aching limbs and splitting head.
Don't see why she should sit and brood
When all I want is drink and food.

She just says 'I've had enough'
When I tell her I've been rough.
I can't see why she complains
I'm the one who's got the pains.

I know they say you shouldn't boast
But I'm harder with myself than most.
So - when people as me 'How's the pain'
You'll hear my saying
Can't complain!

Alan Reid

View From Breightmet Hill

I could spend hours and hours just standing quite still.
Looking down over Bolton from Breightmet Hill.

Wandering slowly through times long gone.
Civil War Battles lost and won.

Popping far bubbles and sparking clogs
Rushing in droves to a hard days slog.

A Sikh selling charms from a battered old case.
Coming fourth at Moss Bank in the egg and spoon race.

Eating butties of condensed milk, sugar or jam,
Playing knock-a -door run, getting done of yer man.

Dew drops in kids noses hanging down to their chests
Forgetting the hankies pinned to their vests.

Afternoon naps on the school room floor.
School clothes from Bowes with the man at the door.

Meeting dates at the library, remember the frill
Three pints at Mayors and feeling right ill.

Founder's then Palais hoping to score
Winklepickers and stilettos on the bouncing floor.

Hanging round Moor Lane wolf whistles and sighs
For girls wearing miniskirts up to their eyes.

The Parish Church and Town Hall in winter's white chill,
Proud memories of Bolton from Breightmet Hill.

Ken Ramsden

Our Environment

Why do we destroy the things we love most
Spoiling a scene so serene,
Why do we crave to dash around
Making life so ugly and mean.

Trees must be free to express their glory
Skies to glow with lovely hue,
Grass encouraged to whisper its story
And the young to enjoy it too.

It's easy to care for the beauty God gave
Preserve some, money can't buy
The feeling inside makes it so worthwhile
We can do it if we try.

Put a little thought in your everyday life
Extra care without frown,
The rewards you'll find with little strife
Are those to be handed down.

There are many blessings in this wonderful world
So much love to be found,
Happiness is there to have and to share
So enjoy it but leave it around.

M Draycott

North West is Best

North West is best,
Beats all the rest,
Land of Lowry's matchstick men
You'll go back again and again.

Sad reminders of days gone by
Cotton mills, cloth caps, people sigh,
When they remember days before TV
Only the radio, the BBC.

Land of Coronation Street
Local pubs, friends all meet
Down to the chippy, for pie and peas
Salt and vinegar if you please.

Wigan Pier is a must
People believe us, only just
That there really is a pier
Have a stroll, take a beer.

Ashton Market is a treat
Opened by Reg, of the Street
Bright and gay with lots of room
Buy a map or a broom.

Manchester Centre
Liverpool Docks,
Old Town Halls
With chiming clocks.

Yes! Northern Folk are just great
Friends forever, with your best mate
I never want to stray or roam
'Cos the North West is my home.

Irene Woodstock

Sight O' Pendle

From my kitchen window,
The view beyond the sill,
A landscaped slope, a school playground,
And distant, Pendle Hill.

My old house, in a terraced street,
I didn't want to leave;
Since I occupied this bungalow,
I've found no cause to grieve.

Before its door was opened,
It had a pull for me;
And meeting kindly neighbours - said
It's where I want to be.

I asked through prayer, for guidance;
Estate agents, I didn't comb;
And exceeding expectations,
Here I am, at Home.

Ivy Squires

View From the North

It's said when travelling northwards
Turning left can be a treat,
For you enter North West England
And there you'll surely meet,
Such a mixing pot of talent
And ideas by the score,
That on looking for the best of life
You couldn't ask for more.

With the sunny sands of Southport,
Bright lights of Blackpool too,
The Liverpool sense of humour
Mancunians whose who,
Granada shines in TV land
The Beeb adds wealth at its command.

Then there's cricket and there's football
Fish and chips of which to dine,
And the Halle and the Opera
For those who have the time,
For culture kick and fashions slick
It really is sublime.

Yes the North West part of England
To say the very least,
With rich ploughed lands and big brass bands
It's really quite a feast
Friendly hands are reaching out
Come on, see what we're about,
Welcome to the North.

Anne Dunseath

Colne Parish Church

My favourite building is the Colne Parish Church, named
St Bartholomew.
It stands near the centre of Old Bonny Colne, founded
eleven twenty two.
It is built on the same hill as old Bonny Colne, right in the town's
main street,
Far, far away above the sea level, six hundred and twenty three feet.
The church tower is sixty two feet high, battlemented and buttressed,
The lower portion is part of the original church, but it has been
rebuilt as the rest.
The interior too is beautiful, west to east hundred and twenty feet.
A nave, three side aisles, two chantries, a chalice, with
stone pillars make it complete.
A font was presented around fifteen-eighteen, by
Lawrence Townley of Burnside.
The font stands four feet, six inches high, basin
eight inches deep, two feet wide.
When the Crimean War was ended, and the news in Colne was
known
The flag on the tower was unfurled to the breeze,
the very first time it was flown.
When the church bells ring they can by heard, nigh on five miles
away
So clear, so mellow, sweet in tone, calling all to pray.
In the grounds are graves of long, long ago, some old fashioned
stocks too.
Come springtime, daffodils bloom all around, making an
enchanting view.
There is such a lot more that I could write, about my favourite
building,
And I can honestly say, it is all quite true, I have not done any
gilding.

Hilda Naughton

Liverpool

I live in a town called Liverpool, a place in the North by the sea,
Where everything's stopped, no work on the docks and
The most of the town just the same.
But the people don't change, their humour the same and
They live with a life full of pride
Even though they are skint and the dole queues are big
They laugh and smile just the same.
These special people of Merseyside are a credit I think to
themselves,
They have nothing like our Regal Queen nothing expensive they
own.
But they carry on living their own little lives enjoying their lives on
the dole.
I love the people of Merseyside, they have something special you
see.
You can travel the world, but one thing you won't find
Our people so friendly and free
Our Merseyside clan are the best in the land so proud so
loveable so true
Our Liverpool town the best you can buy and the best little
town you can find.

Penny Thompson

Old Lanky Local

If I stood outside local, when I were a lass
I could hear happy laughter and clinkin' of glass.
While the men played at cards
All the women a'd talk,
And I'd hear thud on dart board, an scrapin' of chalk.

There were laughin' and shoutin', from all ends a room
Then Lill a'd get up, an' she'd play 'em a tune,
And I'd stand there an' think, I don't know why you bother
'Cos one lot sang one song, and one lot another.
There were clappin' and shoutin' and reet goings on
And old Bill a'd get up and he'd give em a song,
In a voice old and croaky, he'd sing *Nellie Dean*
And I stand there and try to imagine the scene.
All the red happy faces, all yellin' for more,
You'd a thought it were *gigli* from all the encore.

Then at last ten o'clock cum and landlord a'd shout
Time gentlemen please: and he'd chuck em all out.
Thru' the door they'd alla tumble
With shouts of 'Goodneet,'
And, 'I'll see you tomorrow, are you sure you're alreet?'
Then they'd stand and they'd natter half hour or more
Until one by one, they'd all slam their front door,
Then silence would fall like a dark silken hood,
For at last, all the locals we're home
From the pub.

Muriel Altham

Memories

What's happened to old Lancashire
Where the Red Rose flew with pride,
The cobbled streets, the horse and cart
And our trams we used to ride.

Our clogs and shawls were famous
Our cottons and wool's the best,
And our great Lancashire hotpot
Would put hairs upon your chest.

The cotton mills would be working
From early morn 'til night,
We worked long hours but didn't mind
For to us it just seemed right.

To strangers it may seem silly
But we were very proud,
Our neighbours then were all close friends
We were a happy crowd.

When Mum made us rag puddings
We'd run the whole way home,
And if by change she'd flour to spare
She'd make us all a scone.

Those days, alas, are now no more
No horses, carts or trams,
The mills, the clogs, the shawls all gone
Replaced by traffic jams.

Progress or not, as time goes by
There's one thing everyone knows,
Whatever else will come and go
They'll never trample the Rose.

E Senior

The Cheshire Lings

The morning spring, the summer days, the autumn and the fall,
The newness of our first seen sight's, wrapped snugly in a shawl,
A dawn of life, a break of day, the smell of new mown meadow hay,
The starting point, the milk was sour, but life's is rich we have the hour.

Our childhood days, our tender years, the peep of day, we know not tears,
Bedtime becomes our daily task, like tea forever in a flask,
Ghost visions, dreams and fantasy, mirror in our innocent brain,
We feel ourselves like angels, dancing down some primrose lane.

But knee high life soon comes upon us, as we tussle round the floor,
We learn to walk, we learn to talk and ask questions by the score,
Curiosity becomes our knowledge and a wanting for to know,
We ask how things are growing, and how the seeds we sow.

We nose, we peep, we snoop and pry, and ask our parents the reason why,
Attention holds it's vacant eyes, as mother tells here little lies,
Everything living is study bent, regardless of where it came or went,
And the carriage soon will leave the train, as innocent thoughts will leave our brain.

Lack of news is like no words from home, shallowness swell's in us alone,
Darkness brightens our virgin soil, known no better our un'guilty smile
Everyone is super bound, in their youthful days of life,
We over throw our up sets, and high jump our daily strife.

Life's space, life's span is similar, to the universe itself,
And the millstone we tie round our necks was the destiny of self.

Thomas Lawler

The Hidden Gorge

We walked up a gorge which was hidden, unseen,
And found the rock face through a lacework of green.
The river below over boulders was leaping,
Twisting around where tree roots were creeping
Gently, to dip in the water so clear
As it wended its way to a far distant weir.

The sun filtered through to the flowers below,
Tilting their faces to enjoy the soft glow.
The pathway was narrow amid tree roots and ferns,
With parts washed away and hazardous turns.

We stood in a copse to look at the scene
Across Gollinrod Gorge, with the river between.
A little grey squirrel climbed way up on high
In a sycamore tree, as we wandered by.

Such beauty and peace we found on that day
As the old River Irwell went on its way.
The woodland, the silence, was there all around,
No blaring radios, no cans on the ground.
A beautiful place, secluded and rare,
And a challenge to those who venture in there.

Leslie Woods

Rossendale - Lancashire

I have travelled far over hill and vale
Especially during the war.
But there's beauty here in Rossendale
I have never seen before.

The hills around the valley
Proud sentinels they stand,
Keeping a watchful eye upon
This very fine bit of land.

There's beauty to be found in the smile
Of the friendly Lancashire folk,
Who will often stop and chat a while
And maybe crack a joke.

I love the folk, I love the hills
I love those fine green hills.
It was on this fine bit of land
Were many cotton mills.

The women then in clogs and shawls
The men in clogs and cap.
All of them hardworking folk
Before the unemployment trap.

Yet, chin up folks it's not so bad
We still can say with pride,
There's beauty here in Rossendale
If your eyes you open wide.

Joanne McDonnell

Surface Tensions

'Urban decay is here to stay,' is what we like to say.
Kids on the corners of blazing electric streets
With their vandalised burnt out cars.
Drunks spilling out from local bars.
People on the corner with plenty to say, chant
A new rhyme 'McDonalds, McDonalds, Kentucky Fried
Chicken and a Pizza Hut.'

Sitting in a motorway services
You hear the kids order poisoned food
With childlike exclamations of joy.
(because of the free biodegradable toy)
While their mothers and fathers just sit and stare
What the hell do they care?

Urban decay comes from within like a disease
Which feeds on fertile ground and humane people.
Where there once was a town is a city.
Where there once was love is hate.
Console yourself, concrete is pretty.
We don't look too far, not when we speed past in a car.

Kids on the corners of blazing electric streets.
People in endless lines and love doesn't have the power
It once did. 'You are all dole queues, and all social workers, I.'
Drawing out further and further 'til the city
Becomes so pretty on the surface.

Andrew Oldham

Friday Nights

After tea on Friday wer mi favrit time ert week
Ad geet Sam off the *Rose-Grown* an kids of to sleep.
In th' afternoon I'd done mi baking, 12 loaves I'd baked that day.
I'd done mi ironing an put it on t'rack and oisted it up out ert way,
Blackleading ad all bin done as well, wit zebo polish an all.
Then brasso wer used to shine up fender, an fire banked up wi coal.
Doctors chap ad come as well fer is usual tanner a week,

Prudential an coal chap, fert money at th' end ert week.
Afore Sam went off to *Rose an Crown* he'd bring long tin bath in,
It wer kept on th' ook in t' backyard, between t' closet an midden.
Ad fill mi bath wit 't ladin-can-air't ert side boiler, tha noes,
Then ad lock back door wi t' six-inch key, then mi curtains I'd close.

Big fireguard wer then put back place, so I'd put mi clean nightie
on it,
Then I'd geet off rack mi clean combs as well, mi bloomers an
liberty bodice
Thi light ert week wer next to come as I'd fling me close on t'chair,
It wer that blissful feeling wen ah unfastened mi stays
an let mi flesh breathe some air.

Lifebuoy soap wer t' latest thing, it wer a luxury an noa
But Sam liked mi to smell like that wen up to bed wid go.
Bliss! that's way it was, nowt but bliss each week as Friday come
round
Wi weren't well off, far from it tha noas, but wi Sam an t' kids,
Contentment wer summat ad found.

Edna O'Hara

Homecoming

Almost mournful the waves came to rest
Reaching out I touched quick moisten sand.
Falling forward small stones pass my breast
And all returned through my fingered hand.

A lay still, waiting, hoping return
And feel once more sweet moment of birth.
My appointment with Lethe adjourned
I gathered each covering for Earth.

Within each dream was corded a life
Weaving its way through my self made loom
On seeing clearly how storm bird strife
Would gracefully return with full bloom.

If only to catch one's last full breath,
To realise myself from man made dreams.
I died in the sand a thousand deaths
While darkness took me down oceans streams.

In wombed wall my thumb played silent host
Secured in seas of fluid pastures,
Adrift as eternal, timeless ghost
Unconscious of buoyant oak rafters.

Michael David Oram

In Walton Jail

Tracing emptiness in the shape of his face
And his eyes pointing skywards
The silence, heart piercing scream
And the tunnel he's digging.

Walking circular, aimless courtyards
And his feet rock steady
The anguish, the end of a dream
And the tunnel he's digging.

Ursula Curwen

Above Trawden

Out of one window water glints in the sun:
Out of the other rain slants across the pane.
Shelter seeking sheep huddle against dry stone walls.
Reeds lean back from the wind.
Thoughts will not weather
But struggle like a ship driven to rocks, reef then shore
When caption and crew would rather be at sea.

Distant hills change colour as day exhausts itself.
When night falls, few lights show:
A single shaded bulb; smoulder of wood.
In the sparkle of the glass,
Whisky without water,
A hand rise, pauses, puts down
The comfort, without drinking.
Present talk drones on, thoughts elsewhere.
Trapped bodily
In this bleak but beautiful landscape;
Cut off from the phone fax world
Where considerations are.

The land evokes an absence
Absence of everything
Except itself.
A refugee
Even from itself.

Jo Harding

A Summer Rhapsody

Summer stirs.
Swallows, twittering overhead
Retrieve their nesting place.
Trees now have burst their buds of secrecy,
And in abundance
Shade the misty haze of bluebell wood,
The fading semblance of a passing spring.
A beetle,
Still drowsy from its winter sleep,
Explores the bracken fronds
Unfurling to the warmer sun.
Below the fellside's deep descent,
The distant lake,
Where yachts becalmed, lay still,
Sails likened to the scattered fragments
Of a paper chase.
The sun kissed gorse,
A blazoned canopy of gold,
Enticing hovering insects to activity,
Their constant murmurings
A soothing antidote to sleeplessness.
No summer rhapsody could be complete
Without the cuckoo's plaintive overture,
A passing visitor of ill repute,
Yet, in elusiveness,
Delights the listener's ear,
And swells the summer song.

Nancy Morley

Moon Options

I shall hold the moon.
The winds freedom embrace me.
Spangling waters diamond points
Stand still like tears on proud planes of young face,
Before falling into the Earth's green to disappear forever.
Soft clouds cross her face,
Shadowy secrets covering
Tender lips glistening white.
I shall hold the moon like this forever.
Life's struggle continues without my attention.
I shall be a rose sweetly smiling
'Til petals fall gently on a warm afternoon.

E Brooke

Closing Time at the Mill

The goit is high
And black the evening sky.
December's in
And with the wind
Beating, sheeting winter rain
Splatters on the mill-top panes.
The whistle blows.
Body-bent,
The clog-worn people
(Sun-starved people)
Hurry home
To the terrace fireplace, the coal,
And market pies.
(The fire glows
As the engine dies)
Up at six
And to the mill.
Each must clock the picks.

John Norcross

Lancashire People

The old Lancashire people were a down to earth lot
They would share with their neighbours
Most things they had got.
To the pub they would saunter after their tea
To play cards, or dominoes, over a pint or three.
Then late in the evening
Back home they would roam
Putting the world right, as they made their way home.
The kids in their beds, with faces all scrubbed
Ma in the kitchen chopping the wood
Gran in the chair in her old clogs and shawl,
Telling of tales she liked to recall.
Those were the old folk, in days gone by
Content and happy to see the world go by
But today that's all changed, in this modern age,
Yet people are fighting, the worlds in a rage
O how I do wish I could turn back the page.

Barbara Boon

A Lancashire Lorry Driver

I travel all over the country,
There's none of it I haven't seen,
The Southerners heaven, is beautiful Devon,
A Scotsman might say Aberdeen.

But on Friday when I'm heading home,
With just enough fuel in my tanks,
I look for the sign that tells me that I'm
Nearly back in dear Rossendale, Lancs.

This valley's been home to me now,
For all of my forty-odd year,
And when I'm sixty-five, if I'm still alive,
I'll spend every minute right here.

To me it's the friendliest county,
And I know, cause I've been to the lot,
You'll travel some miles and not match the smiles
Of my kin folk, the Rossendale lot.

Brian Taylor

Blackpool Lights

Laughing and singing all the way
The journey only takes an hour,
It's our once a year day
Then all at once we see the tower.
What a wonder
What a sight,
All lit up against the night.
On the coach excitement rises
Children always love surprises,
Little faces pressed on windows
Trying so hard not to sleep
Then they shout and scream
Look it's Bo-Peep with her sheep,
Made of lights, what a scene
Humpty Dumpty
Jack and Jill
All the rhymes we used to know.
If your ever feeling fed up
Blackpool is the place to go.

Bett Thorpe

England My Country

I vow to thee my Country,
I've often heard it said
The beauty of old England
Will live when we are dead.
The spirit of her people
The lonely, rich or poor
Is as high as any steeple
And you will find an open door.
The green fields and the meadows
Are a joy to be seen.
And most of all, without a doubt
We have our lovely Queen.
Then there is the Mersey
Where most of our ships were born
Our proud and lovely Raven bird
Who stands there all forlone.
I'm glad I live in England, I'm glad
That I was born
For there always be an England,
Who could ask for more.

Melda Larsen

My Home County

I'm proud of my home County - Lancashire
It's not all clogs and cloth caps, not at all.
Though somehow people think we talk *real queer*,
We're friendly folk, who love to have you call.

We may like hot pot, pies and tripe and onions,
Fish and chips, a glass of beer or two.
But we work hard and care for all our young 'uns
And wish there was no need for long dole queues.

We've lovely countryside and seaside places,
People come to see, and seem surprised.
They'd imagined all backyards and dirty pavements,
Smoking chimneys, mills, not very nice.

Oh! Yes, we get more rain and winds than sunshine,
At times when it should just be nice and bright.
But we've green fields with buttercups and daisies,
Not dried up grass, and leaves that curl up tight.

We've Blackpool Tower and Morecambe Bay and Southport,
Lovely towns enjoyed by one and all.
Bracing air and fun, with lots of concerts,
And bright *illuminations* in the *fall*.

So when they try to stop us speaking dialect,
That *Lanky Twang* they really think so queer.
I shout aloud - why should I say it quietly -
I'm proud of my home county - Lancashire.

Olive Smith

The Tops

The short climb
takes me past
the parks and people.
A few steps more
reveal the quiet quarries.
A little more time treading rushes
takes me to the moor.

The open moor,
more open than I can describe,
Ii an undulating space
reaching horizontally to the hills and sky
and empty space, apparently,
a fresh element for me
but still the secret home of Falcon and of snipe.

J M Mills

God's Country

If you can talk to God and hear Him,
If you can see Him in the sky.
Please give to Him a message -
Ask Him not to pass me by.

Tell Him sometimes I just need a hand
To lift life's heavy load,
And that I really would appreciate
Some help along the road.

And how He lifts me with the Cheshire Plains,
The Macclesfield hills,
The ripple of the Bolin
With all it's turns and spills.

My thanks for Tatton in the summer,
I could watch the deer all day.
And for helping guide my footfalls
To the next step on the way.

Prestbury village main street
With its conducive atmosphere
There is something wafting in the air
Which says, 'We're glad you're here.'

If there's a heaven on this earth
For somewhere it must be.
It's a long way North of Birmingham.
At least it is for me.

Mike Tolchard

Our Town

Rising neath sweet-chestnut trees
Through many gardens, just to please,
The river Wey goes gently flowing
To join Thames via Godalming.
Round the ponds, where wild swans nest;
And Kingfisher is welcome guest.

With Georgian homes and cobbled ways:
The town is redolent of gentler days;
And down its winding horseshoe hill
Children come trotting from the mill.
Past ancient tavern; and verges wide,
Single file from Blackdown ride.

Come summer, all the township sings
As music of recorder rings,
Harpsichords and viols sound,
Painters flourish; and poets abound.
If one prefers all quiet and peace
The old museum tends release.

There, the trees old parks reveal:
The visions Tennyson made real,
And o'er the ha-ha lambs are seen
Grazing; like snowflakes on the green.
The highest hills stand in the rear
Making a picture of Haslemere.

Mary C Hastie

Summer's Evening on the Beach

Warm air sifts through long hair
And cool winds lift lank locks,
Feet delve into finest sand -
Sand that separates bare toes
Which otherwise, could not bear the touch!
Cotton clothes cling in the breeze -
The feeling of being clothed,
Yet free, at one and the same time -
Walking as on air;
The bubbling sea lapping on chilled paddling feet
And all around the view -
Clear, though appearing distant -
Outlines blur as the sun sinks,
Children's voices softened by the chatter of wavelets,
Dogs revelling in interesting freedom -
The soft ground yielding under strong paws;
There's evidence of picnics, happy hours,
Spent by families, already homeward bound;
Gulls observe and seem to tell all -
From their vantage points on roofs and chimney pots.
Their raucous sound forever conjures up for me another world,
Found only on a beach on summer evening's.

Janet Tapping

The Downs

Towering high over lowlands long,
Chalk Downs stand,
Whose curves and undulations do most typify,
All things pleasant, pure and fine,
In England's ravaged land.

Standing surveying from gusty heights,
Peoples past endeavours,
Whose nibbling charges did reduce,
Great wooded slopes to airy openness.

On the backs of those who came before,
Grows the sweetest sward,
With fragrance that entwines the soul,
Intoxicates with things exotic.

On steepest scarp are shimmering hordes,
Flowers of petite perfection,
While butterflies dance like children's kites,
Confetti in the wind.

Rejoice in all things fine and fair,
Upon the open Down,
For man has tamed the milky maid,
Thwarted thorn and bosky bane,
And set the jewel in England's Crown.

Jonathan Reburn

Sunrise

Glimmering, at first, like a candle, on the eastern horizon,
Sunlight grows.
Spears of amber burst on to bloodstained skies,
Stretch out across fertile fields of wheat and barley,
Over chalk downs where people once longed to go on pilgrimages,
Past St. Martha's church in the distance,
Blessing the wooded Chantries and Pewley Hill,
Where the castle tumbles down on the steep slopes
Of the High Street and the valley below,
Where the slow Wey winds silently over meadows,
Over the railway station,
Beyond bridges and tunnels and viaducts of stone,
Glistening on the tall spire of St Saviour's Church;
And away from the still of the city,
Its drowsy congregation of houses,
Innumerable inns, countless shops and concrete offices,
Out to the ruins of St. Catherine's,
Overlooking the religious river,
To a bare cottage or a snug outline of a farmhouse,
Where shrubs in plots and allotments tremble under an empty sky,
Over dappled hedges where bushes cluster in rustling thickets,
Above the rise of Stag Hill,
Where the erect edifice of the sturdy cathedral impressively stands,
Sweeping over holy hills,
Climbing to the Mount
And penetrating far into the west,
Transfiguring the white-limbed birch:
The earth prepares its body for the perfect communion.

D W Fincham

A Glimpse of West Sussex

The view from glorious Goodwood
Or Slindon so fair,
Enchants each happy wanderer
Whose feet have trodden there.

Look South to the horizon
Where the Channel meets the sky,
Or westwards to Chichester
There's more to meet the eye.

To the East lie peaceful villages
Viewed from Chanctonbury Ring,
While below sits Bognor Regis
A town fit for a king!

From the windmill at Halnacker
On a clear day you can see,
The Roman Palace at Fishbourne
Bosham Harbour and Dell Quay.

In Arundel there's a castle
And the Arun that flows to the sea,
Follow its banks to discover
The joys of Pulborough and Amberley.

Medieval cottages
Churches centuries old,
Acres of woodland
And cornfields of gold.

The toil of generations
Have shaped this County, and
Just as far as I'm concerned
It's the best in all the land!

Norah Sansom

Milland Church - West Sussex

'What is a church?
No! Please, do not rush by but
Stay awhile, I pray,
What is a church? I say.'
'What is a church? Well . . .'
'Listen, whilst I describe my church to you.'

As you rush along the busy A3, cast your eyes aside.
On the left, a little woodland ride
A clearing through the trees
Four walls, a roof, a space below,
This is the church which I love so.
A quiet place - I am all alone.
A meeting place - I am never alone.
A simple place, but this, you see,
Is where I can truly get to know me.
My busy life I leave for a while -

Ah, now I see you smile,
You are on your way.
Remember me and remember too,
That somewhere there is a space for you.

Anne Leahy

Ighthan Mote

Ightham Mote - the epitome of a Medieval Moated Manor.
Mysterious, magic and magnificent
At all seasons.
Sparkling in a sudden springtime shower,
Shimmering in the midday sun of summer,
Melting into the mists of an autumn morning
Or merging in the shadows of a moonlit winter midnight.
Mysterious, magic, but in no way menacing.

Virginia Trease Garrett

Dunwich Lament

The grave of poor John Easy
Will surrender to the sea,
Cruel waters of Dunwich
Erasing history,
Once you were a proud town
Your coffers rang with gold,
Until the east wind
Swept your heart away
And the north sea
Took your soul.

The old ones
Can still tell you
Of all Saints, where they prayed
Until the crumbling cliffs
Took their church,
And even took their graves,
Will the tears of grief ever end?
Will the tempest ever be?
Until Dunwich is a memory
Taken by the sea.

Sometimes the bells of Dunwich
Beneath the sea still ring,
The waves join in the chorus
And the wind begins to sing,
Then fishermen upon the sea
Will point their boats to shore
And offer up a plaintive prayer
To stop that mighty roar.

When I walk along your shore line
Or stand upon your cliffs,
My heart goes out to Dunwich
For the tragedy you've lived,
Maybe it's time to leave you
To the fate that must befall,
When the final storm begins
And the cruel sea takes your all.

J N Cates

My Own Dear Garden of England

I've travelled far from Hull to Ghent
But in my blood there's always Kent.
So let us then our tracks turn into
And through that County make our journey.
Like Chaucer's pilgrims we begin our hike
Along the way the Pardoner took
To see brave spires before us then
As for Canterbury our way we wend
So much to see, so far, so wide
Our boat 'neath river's tunnel glide.
Let's have our fill, prolong the stay
Then journey back, 'long Pilgrims Way.
Next stop is Maidstone's County Hall
It needs a day to see it all
So have a bite next Archbishop's Palace
Then see bridges lift unto their marriages
In nearby old Museum of Carriages.
Next cross the Downs past Upper Bell
The road descends - I know it well.
Hark. can't you hear Cathedral's bell?
Yes, Rochester, Charles Dickens home
To city great our tourists come
And High Street fills with folk galore
To witness sights that author saw
So join the crowd, let's go and see him
And enter city's old museum.
There's much to see, so much unsung
Alas our travelling's nearly done
Next time you are on journey bent
Come join with us in dear old Kent.

Cyril Saunders

A Summer Shower

The summer heat has lasted long,
The lillies droop their curly stems,
Their pollen falls like golden gems
Glistening on the daisy throng.
The blackbird sings a shorter song,
And lingers on the shaded hems
Of dressy shrubs with diadems
Where sparkling raindrops should belong.
The garden wilts, so tired of sun,
It longs for gentle, kindly rain
To swell its beating heart again.
'Is that a cloud at last?' it sighs,
'Perhaps a summer shower's begun'
It raises high its hopeful eyes.

J I Wilson

The Coming

The coming of dawn
Ripening corn,
The low heat haze
Happy days.
The sound of larks
Green fertile parks,
Lazy streams
Midsummer dreams.
Those halcyon days are gone
Memories still linger on,
The earth cools
Pollution rules.

P Norris

Walking in My Mind

My rooting feet
        Once tramped
Your ways of loveliness,
        But now the confined
Narrows of this room
        Enable me to leap
From hill to shining hill,
        Or find the depths
Of deep, deep darkness
        In your secret lakes.
There is no limit
        To walking in my mind.
I see the dusty sanctity
        Of echoing worship where
High windows of light
        Are traced again with joy.
I watch the binding chains
        Of ceaseless traffic,
Each little box a prison cell,
        And turn aside to healing
Greenness, and quiet paths
        To dappled dells
And sudden flights of distance.

Peter Stock

July 1993

Living in an isolated town
in an isolated country
No, living in an isolated body
I have grown to be many ages old.

In my loneliness I listen to shrieking voices
that echo from a distant place
where no men live nor die.

A hundred souls on a hundred drums
eternally beat out an incoherent rhythm
for the dancing blue-silk sheets,
forever stained by the products of our imagination.

Yes, it is the corpse of a thirsty giant
that feeds the spirit of this broken land
where only shadow-people live.

Sex, love, love lost and sex not gained
gradually grow unimportant
For I dreamily slip in and out of reality,
slowly discovering my place in the world.

And as my mother cries:
'I always knew that you weren't mine -
that you belonged to something greater'
I climb my way into the heavens
while the angel holds the ladder.

Scott Carman

Impressions of Sussex

Trundling down the Brighton Road,
I see a spectral cavalcade -
Straggling families daubed with wode
In silhouette against the golden sky -
Travelling on ancient paths
Across the shoulders of the Downs.

The echoes of the pack *in tongue*
I smell the fear of driven fox:
I hear the wind in soughing sound
Through trees primeval - now turned
Into battleships and charcoal, and cooked stew.

The onion skins of history
Unpeel with meditation -
The stench of plague and cesspits foul,
The fear and vibrations which soil the earth
Soaked by blood, spilt in name
Of religion, politics, and fame.

The slash and grumble of unrelenting waves
Attacking the edges of rolling beach -
The pleasant lapping, trickling
On days of sun and balmy breeze.

The lichen, grass green and ochre,
Growing inevitably on the cow shed roof
Of pantiles - and crashing to the ground
By the weight of its own success.

The laughter of human children,
And the joyous coupling of the slightly grown -
The promenade of older feet
And memories of personal days.

Thelma Welham

A Canterbury Tale

I beat on the Cathedral door,
'Thomas, are you there?' I cried,
But no voice replied
To rend the fabric of the heavy air.
No footsteps echoed on the stone floor
Within, or on the ancient, tower stair.

'Thomas, I have no companion by my side.
Alone, I travelled the path the pilgrims trod
In search of Truth and God.'
But silence answered my despairing call,
And it was the wind that sighed
And whistled, not human breath at all.

I was about to turn away, when
Not from behind the forbidding door,
Where blood was spilt on marble floor,
But from between the trees
A voice did calmly speak and then
Was carried to me on the breeze.

'Why stand you at this empty portal?
Why did you tread the path the pilgrims trod,
In search of Truth and God,
When they are not here, but in your heart,
And the immortal Truth in all things mortal
Rests, and the divine, the whole of nature does impart.'

T'was by these words, not pilgrimage, my soul was healed.
I will no longer seek the Truth in worn-out creeds,
No longer plead
With long dead saints. I turned my gaze from the Cathedral tower.
No longer blind, I saw God revealed
In nothing more mysterious, more sacred, than a flower.

Litsa Close

Surrey Hills

Seasons in my air-conditioned cell
merge into a seamless uniform;
screens and lights my masters, they will tell
me - press a switch, encounter dusk or dawn.

Coppered autumn gently steals the scene
from summer's ample tapestry of green.

Submerged, dark caffeine keeps me half awake
while daydreams leave ambitions unfulfilled
and mutter, 'Take the train and make
your southbound journey to the Surrey Hills.'

Chalk lined strata from another time
where wildly-scented honeysuckles climb.

Twice a week the florist comes to tend
her potted plants, obediently trained:
'They say it's going to be a wet weekend!
Will you be going home?' 'I love the rain

on Headley Heath - with scabious in bloom!
The Surrey Hills!' I call across the room.

Anita Holmes

Memories of Childhood

I was born in Sussex County at a village in the downs
Where a million wild flowers grew and hills wore trees as crowns.
Hidden from the outside world for years there as a child,
gave one faith in nature both tame and running wild.

To dream there it was easy wherever you may lie,
breeze touched leaves in all the trees and sang a lullaby.
Gardens overflowing, fruit ripened on the vine,
blue skies dried the washing dancing on the line.

Butterflies were all around, birds graced the sky above,
to the flowers mid the green, bees hummed a song of love.
Hills embraced the village, together it did bind
all the village people, lives all intertwined.

West Dean you were home to me in those long gone days
of village life and village love and Sussex County ways.
Near and far I've travelled since and turned life's many keys,
but I've still a happy mindful of childhood memories.

J Whitmarsh

London

The glory of London has girdled the earth
And her sons have spread the fire of her fame
Many men of many lands
Have feared and revered her name.

But in the end time conquers all,
And the mightiest empires' fail and fall,
Yet by that very self same token
Wherever English is still spoken
London may remembered be.

London my home - my own County.

M Parker

Summer Sunday on a Sussex Beach

Nose to tail, in stifling heat we queued,
Trapped in our metal boxes, tempers frayed,
Longing to reach our goal, the golden sands,
The sparkling waves, the picnic spread, the Sunday treat.

Arrived, the car disgorged us, eager now
To join the jostling crowd, the sun-soaked throng.
Dog slipped its lead, I stumbled in pursuit,
Leaping the limbs spread-eagled like a maze,
Dodging the stones flung carelessly at cans,
Stifled by stench of seaweed, sun oil, beer.

Dog captured and restrained from Channel swim,
Dragged yapping, scrabbling, over rattling stones.
I searched the sea of faces. Panic struck.
No kids. No sign. Just strangers all around.
But then, relief! a small hand touched my arm.
A sandy sandwich offered with a grin.

Yet still I fretted, fraught with worldly cares,
Fighting contentment, wrapped in self-made stress.
I came for peace. I needed space to breathe,
To cool my burning body, fevered brain.

Into the waves we rushed with shrieking glee,
Plunging through breakers spraying sunlight surf.
Far out I swan to calm, cool, greener deep;
Floated, relaxed, and felt the tension ease.
The swell caressed me gently, soothed my soul.
The sea was mine, the space, the happiness.

Revived, restored, I called the kids for games,
Smiling my thanks for dripping ice-cream cone.
God's gift to man, a summer seaside scene.
I will return again to share the joy it brings.

F B Gibberd

The South Downs

The South Downs lift like a wave from the sea,
Their gentle crest swelling more and still more,
Then with a swoop of exhilaration,
Steeply plunging down to the valley floor.
Light grasses sway and ripple in the wind,
It has shaken off the weight of the sea,
Verdant pastures cover the old sea floor,
A mantle of seasonal tapestry.

Purple orchids stand ramrod straight on guard,
Blue harebells dance to the tune of the breeze,
Whilst the cowslips cluster by downland path,
And white-eyed daisies stare from clumps of trees.
The celestial skylark heading sunwards,
Filling the blue void with its tender song.
A sharp eyed hawk waits motionless, hovering;
Hunter and hunted both hear the sweet song.

In the distant haze the seal lies glinting,
Smiling serenely, waiting not in vain,
The sea waits, sending long snaking fingers,
Ever stretching to take the land again.
But never caring, the Downs roll eastward
Until the sea stands in its way once more,
Grass, flowers, trees, gone in a spray of chalk,
As the great green wave breaks upon the shore.

Barbara Long

Croydon

Even the stones yawn
it is not raining
a train goes by.
Synchronised stiletto typists fade from view
the grass has died of boredom
fairfield gardens - no games allowed.
Below me, a car park
above me, the sky
it occurs to me that the easiest way to kill a man,
is to take him to the latter half of the twentieth century
and leave him in
Croydon.

Chris Alchin

Conservation South East

Ploughing fields with heavy horses
The chains of heavy horses clanging
The munch crunch of the machine,
Looking back at the clean ploughed soil.

What joy the scene gives
The farmer so proud and relieved
Sunset comes forth at the end of the day
The field totally changed and reseeded.

Wonder of time giving change to the day
Whatever comes forth from unknown forces
Birds, badgers, rabbits, mice and foxes
All forms of life going their way.

Tall trees with shimmering leaves
Winds whipping branches right down low
Rustling atmospheres hushing whispers
Quiet peace which silences show truth.

Come share these glorious gifts
Melt away life's worries
Nature continually refurbishes
Washes away untold histories.

These former sights becoming so popular
Organic farming growing in practice
Surely we owe this to the future
Now's the time for honest prudence.

Pamela Searchfield

Sussex Downs

'Gentle climb to beauty, from ancient town below.
Your generous curves enchant the heart of me
And make me long to reach the top and see
Lewes, in all her glory!
Spread out before me.
Give me the gentle curves
Of dreamy Sussex downs
Tenderly rolling and unfolding
Calm and serene, ever still.
Peace tranquil and sublime.
Greeting you as a friend
If to the Downs
Your presence you lend.
Nestled in valley and etched from the Downs
This Lewes survives and nature
Crowns her beauty, mellowed with age.
Forever captured, the Lewes of yesteryear
Walks side by side with modern day living
Each taking a little, one from the other.
Shades of martyrs burned, remembered
In stone, gaze sombrely down. This Lewes
Still is a figure of pride
Taking it all in her stride.

Kay Bailes

Sussex Countryside

Leaving Chichester behind me heading North;
I pass by the golf course . . . velvet smooth, nearby beech trees
nudge the sky.

This place is called *Target Bottom*
Who could have named it, and I wonder why?

By the Goodwood Grandstand is a small wood.
I'm told, no birds sing in these trees, just the winds sigh,
A dark deed was committed here one night.
What was it? and, I wonder why?

Climbing the *Trundle* to gain a view,
The Isle of Wight rewards the keen-ed of eye,
Cowslips dance here to the tune of the Skylark,
Their favourite haunt is the Downs, I wonder why?

Down through the plantations is West Dean Park
Wild daffodils grow nearby,
My denim jeaned daughter and friends counted them,
It's done every year, I wonder why?

The Lavant Course whispers under the bridge at Singleton,
As thought expected some reply.
In the meadow a harrow and roller chime their answer,
I wonder what is was, and why?

Cucumber Farm is just due North,
The remains of a twelfth century hunting lodge now here lie,
The site long carpeted by green shoots,
I shall not leave Sussex; no need to ask *me* why.

B Mills

Guildford High Street

Today the gold sun shines
on this street enclosing
my time, this day.

Generations have known
the street's steep concave slope
on the east-west track
and the north-south highway,
have noticed sun and shade
dividing up its length.

The sundial on the wall
high in the sunlit north
beyond the Angel Gate,
instructs humanity
to learn to tell the time.
Look up. The south's shade won't
expose you as you stand.

Then as you climb, wonder
at the ancient rising roofs
and the Guildhall clock
(whose maker wanted work)
hung out above the street.

A further rise reveals
Archbishop Abbot's place,
gateway and domed turrets,
four gilded weather vanes
aloft. And in the street,
striding the crest, schoolboys
dwarf you as they come
much pleased with prospect down
of flowers, façades and life.

Margaret Dickson

Sussex

In Sussex you are never far from the sea -
Its influence is everywhere:
I have seen corn in late August
Bend to the rhythms of its salty breath,
And screaming gulls from Pagham
Blown inland to waken villages
Borrowed from Doomsday.
I have seen fishermen at Selsey Bill
Mending their nets, their veins
Full of sea shanties.
I have stood at Bosham, in the shadow
Of Canute, and watched multitudes of geese
Filling the air with their nocturnes.

I brought home shells from Church Norton,
And when I long for the sea
I hold them to my ear
And drown in their senses.

Sheila Fisher

Sketching in Knole Park

How warm the air,
How sweet the smell of summer;
Round my feet the insects climb thin stalks of grass-
Miniature pampas plumes waft fragrance,
Dry distillation of long sunshine hours.

How soft the shadow on the trees
Viridian, ochre, Indian red.
The filbert fans soft hairs to comb a haze
Where cattle stir beneath the leaves
And flick their tails or shake an ear.
The paint dries on the palette.
Now thick impasto
Building clouds of cream
Grey-bellied, luminous,
Now thinner paint
To sketch faint roofs of house and school
Spreading across the canvas
The image grows:
Malachite and rose
Scumbled and spread
Fading to distant line of hills.
Oh, to catch the magic breath of August
For shorter days
And colder nights
Will sadden the sweet hopes and dreams of summer.
Frail paint and brush
Must snare
My share
Of this warm day
To glow when winter comes.

Janet Lawrence-Wilson

Country Colours - Ground Frost

Our Lady of Ketton looks down from her window
And sees the stone houses, the fields and the farms,
'How lovely to live in the country, my sunshine,'
She says to the child that she holds in her arms.

The traffic goes by and the people not caring,
Until at the sunrise of one Easter Day,
They see that the light has gone out of the window.
'But where has the little old boy gone?' They say.

'Perhaps it's a power cut,' Our Lady suggested,
'But he will be here with the wine and the bread.
Have you not heard on your radio station?
This week's special offer:
Redemption,' she said.

Beryl Willson

View of a Cathedral

(Salisbury, July 1977)

Those steeplejacks up the spire recline like dummies
In fixed positions on cables. They stiffly sway
Or, in limpet concrescence, cling.

Yet one, I see, can crawl. He has joined the other,
And arms flail busily. Something is being achieved
In those cross-patterned mouldings of stone.

Their tactics appear haphazard. The crawler performs:
The recliner, perhaps, instructs - unless his role
Is purveyor of moral support.

The spire in its Gothic splendour seems detached,
Its dignity unimpaired - not ashamed that its grace
Should depend on those insect men.

Ruth Marden

The Sussex Scene

How great is the South Downs
With fields all around
Looking so green and glorious brown.
Close by a race course, and
As people gather round -
To see the horses win or lose
Maybe with a frown.
Ladies in their best array
With men looking jaunty in
Different hats and coloured shirts.
Not far away is the channel
To the joy of sailors with their dinghy
Windsurfers on the crest of the waves
The gulls screeching and flaying far away -
Far out on gleaming waters
The ride over surging spray
Where winds are blowing free
Not far away is the Majestic castle
Standing amongst the stately trees
With wild life flying round
And ducks all a flutter on the lake close by -
Delighted little children feeding the swans
As they swim by.

Kathleen Le Mare

South Coast Wind

Where does this wind come from?
When out walking it's a job to get along.
The trees bend over,
Let's take for cover
The flowers don't like it
Neither we one little bit
So where does the wind come from . . .?

The coastal towns suffer badly,
As the wind blows madly,
No matter what age you are
It catches you unaware.
The cats don't like it,
They won't go out at night.
So where does the wind blow from?

Ever blowing, ever rushing, mixing the leaves
Dashing, lashing, crashing and bashing underneath the eaves.
The chimneys howl
Possibly a loose cowl
The dogs bark nightly
and houses creak slightly.
So where does the wind hail from?

When all is said and done,
And peace comes at last to some.
Quiet at last,
Gone is the past.
We can now go out
Without any a doubt
Where has the wind now gone . . .?

Donald Maltby

The Garden of England

I've lived in a beautiful garden
For sixty one years or more
Where skylarks sing in the meadows
And seagulls swim by the shore.
On chalky white cliffs looking over to France,
Dainty blue butterflies flutter and dance.
With the smell of the sea and the countryside blending
It brings me such peace and joy never ending.
A beautiful haven indeed Heaven sent
This garden of England, the County of Kent.

J H Sutton

Medway

Loquacious water ambling,
Through Kent's lush green vale;
The places you pass,
The people you meet,
Oh! what a tale you could tell
Of Chafford and of Penshurst
Your neighbours by and by
From Forest Row to Rochester,
Your darting waters sigh.

M J Worsell

Summer Long

On a sunny day,
down by the sea,
looking so calm and serene.
The clear blue sky,
children paddling in the sea.

Ice cream to keep you cool.
So much to do.
Like a busy bee,
buzzing from flower to flower.

The walks along the downs
leave you spellbound.
For miles around,
the views' are breathtaking.

It's so nice to be
by the sea.
In quaint and charming,
Bognor Regis.

Joyce Redman

Untitled

Golden fields of corn, ablaze with scarlet poppies,
Waving in the gentle breeze to the passers by.
Hill upon hill of glorious view to all who pass through
And stop to observe the breathtaking sight of fields
In everlasting green where among the acres of land
A peaceful wood stands, with millions of bluebells
Coloured in soothing blue.
A nightingale sings sweetly, its shrill haunting melody
Echoing above the tall, sheltering trees that touch the sky.
I see the wondrous nature when I am on my travels,
In my dear county, where I am proud to be.

Tracey Kemp

Stonehenge Thoughts

Oh! Silent stones, in circle round -
Your shadows cast upon the ground,
What mysteries you hold, within your heart,
What tales of days gone by, could you impart.

Awesome and majestic, you stand so upright -
A place of deep feeling, on a silent night,
A place of dread, 'midst your circle therein,
So quiet, so still, only the movement of night's vermin.

As I stand alone, 'neath your moon made shade -
I seem to hear voices chanting, yet I am not afraid -
For it seems to be in place, here 'mongst shadows,
The chanting coming louder, echoing from the old barrows.

The silence falls once more, and all is still,
The wind softly moaning, through these stones on the hill,
I look around me, with a wonder in my heart,
How long is your history, and when did it start.

So many tales have been told, of your days,
Folklore has been written, in many changing ways,
But only you, stones of silence, grace and bliss -
Can put a true answer, to tales such as this.

Dennis J Cannings

Lament for a Town Garden

There I embraced her, leaning, naked and so forlorn
Which was once erect and standing tall,
Patiently enduring all.
That changing times and seasons call.
At her feet on a cold bright morn
The fragile snowdrop again was born,
And in springtime on a cheerful, blustery day
The frilled daffodils just seemed to play.
Now clothed in ivy and leaves of green
Sweet honeysuckle and roses most supreme
Home of the blackbird and humming bee
A shady bower she provided me;
But heavily laden and aged now
The winds of winter brought her down
No more she stands amidst the lawn
The old Pear Tree - her loss I mourn.

Barbara E Higgins

Sunset Over Pevensey Marshes

Alone one evening I watched the sun
Shedding its fiery pall
Hanging below the darkening clouds
Like an incandescent ball.

Slowly, slowly it dipped towards
The line of a distant hill
And the salt sea air, like gossamer,
Was waiting, quiet and still.

Beachy Head stood in silhouette
Now that the day was done,
And gilded was the countryside
As deeper glowed the sun.

Colours changed and shadows formed
The sun was lost to sight,
And earth and sky were dipped in dark
As they settled to the night.

I turned from watching the sunset hour
And tears I could not hide,
For I felt a kind of sadness
As the long day gently died.

Then over me in the afterglow
Contentment slowly crept,
As I dreamed and planned for tomorrow
While the silent marshes slept.

Jean Bourchier

Goodbye Jack

She waved goodbye so often, Jack,
Across so many years,
But she never did get used, Jack,
To the sadness or the tears.
When your ship left Pompey harbour, Jack,
She watched from on the shore,
As you sailed on navy business, Jack
To some godforsaken war.
To Jutland or Trafalgar, Jack,
Or to the China Seas,
She said a silent prayer, Jack,
To bring you home safe please.
But now those days are gone, Jack,
You'll sail from her no more,
Your loyalty all forgotten, Jack,
Your courage just ignored.
It's strange to think that peace, Jack,
Will be the death of you,
When you fought so many wars, Jack,
And always saw them through.
So a fond farewell forever, Jack,
And a last safe voyage too.
Remember Pompey harbour, Jack
As she remembers you.

Tim Bland

Romney Marsh

Imagination stirred by
thoughts of smugglers past,
their shadows make haste
across the marsh,
to distant Inn with
beckoning light.
Marsh churches stand musky, alone,
serene, but for the sheep.
Church echoes the past of
happy wedlock rites.
A ghostly glow from far off
lighthouse,
bats flying swiftly
in its silvery beam.
Pylons stand out against the sky
like giant scarecrows.
Unending flat land, no shady
tree.
Winding roads to nowhere,
past the nonchalant sheep.

Margaret Potter

Ave Mater Anglia

(Lines written in Canterbury Cathedral)

Drop in on Mother when you have the time
Shell be delighted.
A wonderful old lady, well-preserved.
Not one of us will wear the years as she does.
Old fashioned now, of course, and sadly out of touch.
Life has receded from her.
Leaving an echoing emptiness mementoes cannot fill.
Her gaunt hands, still beautiful, lie chilly on us.
She does not give the reassurance that we search for.
The pride that once was hers, the glory and the shame
No longer move her.
Deep within she hides her memories of the days
her children came from need not duty.
Only one solace now wakes her old heart to joy -
Boys' careless voices, singing.
We admire her treasures but do not confide.
Peck her cheek kindly as you leave her,
Unwarmed with nothing said.

Beryl Bull

My England - Just - South East

Hamlets and cities
villages and towns,
factories and inns
rolling grassy downs.

Some roads lead to London
some lead to the sea,
some down leafy lanes
all enrapture me.

Hills now echo joy
once sounds of war,
happy now Hells Corner
Peace endures once more.

Autumn's sepia sun
Spring, a floral show,
Winter's white retreat
Summer's yellow glow.

See saplings, awesome oaks
lilies by a pond
crescendo, Dover Cliffs
need I look beyond.

Placid English pearl
such a rustic feast,
born and pray I die here
My England - Just - South East.

John Wharton

Garden of England

Splinters of glass
Constantly surface
Amongst the roses;
Fragments, reminders,
Refusing burial.
How many panes
Did this house have,
                    I ask.
How many bombs
Rained down.

Helen Allison

Kentish Treasures

If you want to have a break from work and toil
Travel to the South-East, from London or beyond!
There you will find treasures galore
From fields and pastures to sunny shore,
You will find everything you'll ever need.
Orchards abound with fruit trees and cattle;
There's hops to help *make a bottle*,
Corn and vegetables abound in the seasons.
Then there's the Thames and Medway rivers,
The Stour as well, with streams and bridges.
And what of the towns to visit as well,
Canterbury, with its tales to tell that has stood through the ages.
Dickens' Rochester too, abound with stories,
And these are just a few of Kent's glories.

Eleanor Cudd

Untitled

The morning dew lay soft and new
Amidst the surrounding calm.
All around a humming sound
Enlivened summer's charm.

As we strode out, all about
The larks burst into song.
The sun beat down, the falcon soared,
Romance was feeling strong.

Love blossomed in the summer breeze
Sheer beauty and budding growth.
The swaying corn, the restless trees,
I reached out, embraced them both.

The radiance in my lover's smile
Caused heartbeats fast no sense of time.
Still I could feel in a short while
That I would be in life's rich prime.

For she did stir within my soul
A feeling so divine and whole
That all was mine for to control
And heaven shined down upon me.

C J Norton

An Ode to the Conquest

I suppose that day Duke William was feeling a bit down,
You see he'd learned that Harold of England had taken his crown.
So he gathered his forces and best trained Knights,
And they worked all day and they even worked nights.
To build all those boats and weapons and stuff,
To wage war against Harold they had to be tough.
Meanwhile back in England, young Harold, a warrior brave,
Was wearing his crown and giving a wave,
To the messenger who had just arrived at his court,
'A'hve got some bad news Sire!' the messenger said,
'Duke William, they reckon, is seeing quite red,
'Cos you've got the crown he reckons is his
He thinks the whole affair is one big swiz.'
'Does he now,' said Harold out loud.
'In that case, we'll gather an army of which to be proud!
We'll give them Normans the big *E*
That doesn't mean *E* for England, it means Exit, you'll see.'
Well they travelled all night without a respite,
As the journey was what you would call long,
By the time they got there, the weather was fair,
But Harold's army wasn't feeling so strong.
So they set up camp, right there and then,
And decided to have them a brew.
Now Duke William, he was no fool,
He thought and he knew just what to do,
'We'll attack now while they're having a break
Come on lads, let's give them some stick, just remember
what's at stake!'
At long last the battle was over, Duke William had won the day,
While Harold, an arrow in his eye, lay as cold as the clay.
Of how William had done it my friends is no mystery,
'Cos it's written as what they call History!

D Reavely

Nostalgia - Highfields Leicester

Streets are mean, as into rain
Come call girls, tall in their shoes,
Bleeding like tattoos
Low life crawls below the blocks,
Lurking in shadows cast from nineteenth century *Gothic*
Condoms, needles and smashed glass.

In the 1920's, distant galaxies,
Sparkled sequins of stars,
Long past midnight:
Parties spilled out like breasts,
Conquests on cool verandas,
The hum of cars,
Windows bathed in light of chandeliers,
And wide eyed flappers peered,
Sleek behind silk-bobbed hair with kiss curls
Pencil thin, those girls, doing whatever it is
They did to Jazz.

Victoria Park's an emerald jewel against it all
The grime-grey jungle of noiseless dark.
Timetables - warriors lurk
As nightfall casts her confidential cloak
On secrets too big for student bedsits.

Past wading through books
Undergrads hunt in packs, like wolves,
Gripped in talk, dazzling into early morning,
High on dope, whispering, laughing.
The jokes, the booze, the sex,
The highs and lows of education.
A last train rumbles through its way
From Leicester Station.

Sue Osborne

Guernsey

Nestling above the sea,
The Island waits.

As once she waited high above the land,
A hill, a mountain, magnificent,
And awed by friends below.
Now those friends below are only fish.
As creeping fingers of the sea
Rose up to claim the coloured fields
Ice melting at a distant pole.

Now an island,
Helpless she watches her enemy,
Surrounding her now,
Teasing the frills of her skirt,
Wanting to dominate her, cover her, claim her.

Still she waits.
Knowing that soon her time will come.
When she will struggle, not strong enough,
And will slowly drown in the sea's gaping jaws.

For now, she has to provide, protect, and feed.
Secretly she mourns for life lost to the sea.
She will not give in
For all she's worth she will try to stay,
Nestling above the sea.

Nicola Hastings

A Channel Gale

The wind whips the spray from
off the sea,
And lashes it at your face
and knees.
You stagger along the fringe of
the foam,
And collect the drift-wood to
carry home.

In the cottage which faces out
to sea,
You'll have a wood fire and
muffins for tea.
And listen to the roar of the
gale,
As the shutters rattle, and
the chimney wails.

Then in the night the foghorn
will moan,
As the lighthouse guides the
sailors home.
You snuggle down in your cosy
bed,
While the Channel - over all -
its vengeance sheds.

Isabella Fagentees

Folkestone Here We Come

The car feels hot and sticky,
The windows stuck on *shut*,
The sea seems all too far away
Did we have to bring the mut!

But here we are again,
On our happy *Summer hols*,
The car is packed to bulging point,
'Where's that toffee rolled?' who knows.

At last . . . 'I've seen the sea!'
That old familiar shout,
The seaside shops filled to the brim,
The same old 'lager lout.'

'Well who's for fish and chips?' says dad,
'Oh yuck!' came the reply,
I turned to see who dare decline,
As the *toffee* hurtled by!

As mum unpicked the *gooee* mass,
Now resting on her skirt,
Dad and I returned with chips,
Plus gherkin for Uncle Bert!

A well fed sigh - was next to come,
Our thoughts then turned to sand!
The sun hats perched upon our heads,
A bucket in each hand!

Well this is what its all about,
The sea - the sand - the lollies,
The sticks of rock and mugs of tea,
The sounds of *Buddy Holly*.

Deckchairs parked upon *the leas,*
Hotels lean towards the breeze,
Baby's crawl on chubby knees,
Who said 'it takes a lot to please?'

Karen Lawrence

The Hoppers of Kent

The fields in May are quietly dressing
Their barren poles in ragged rows,
Each like a bride sweetly possessing
Fresh garlands, as the green shoot grows.

The plants are trained to climb each string
In May-time sun and showers,
The golden hops a wondrous thing
When bines sprout forth their golden flowers.

The men on stilts they pace the field
To reach the wires on high,
And test the poles to bear the yield
That the harvest will inspire.

Whole families came from London town
None highbred or of social note,
But *hopping's* the thing to bring 'em down
Earning the price of a winter coat.

This was for them a summer treat
The country and a hopper's shed,
(No beach or sea to cool their feet)
A pile of sacks for a makeshift bed?

Blackberry pie and spuds to bake
Black-stained hands and wasps that sting,
Bottled tea and sweet plate-cake
Formed our day around the bin.

The binmen filled the pokes quite full
Of Kentish hops with pungent scent,
High stacked a cart the horse must pull
Back to the oasts of garden Kent.

Brian C Gamage

Home in Sussex

From Greater London I had come
When we were newly wed,
In Middlesex we'd made a home,
Then lived in Hertfordshire instead;

But Sussex was beyond, beyond
The counties that I knew,
Of Crawley I could not be fond.
I'd rather go straight through

To Littlehampton - there's a place
That I held very dear:
The funfair, beach, the grassy space
For children's outings, year by year!

Or *Doctor* Brighton, fresh and bright,
For shopping, just the place to be.
The pier is open free each night.
(Another's falling in the sea.)

But now I've lived in Crawley Town
For fourteen years and more;
They messed it up, we've run it down -
Rubbish and roundabouts galore.

And yet this town to me is dear
For it holds all I need.
Both countryside and town are near,
Its flowers and trees a joy indeed.

Best of all places I have seen
In this green county, high and low,
Is Highdown Hill, I love it still,
Where fresh the wind and grasses blow.

Valerie A Ward

Coggeshall in My Day

Goggeshall is my day was a friendly little place,
No murders, scandals and the like, a smile was on it's face.
The shops were full of goodies, not antiques everywhere
There was fruit, and sweets and groceries and folk had time to stare.
The windows of the shops were bright with tasteful window-dressing
No housing adverts to be seen it really was a blessing.
Coggeshall in my day was a happy little town
No vandals or graffiti to make us wear a frown
The shopkeepers were caring, my dad was one of these
He let poor folk have things on *tick* to bring a bit of ease.
The village of the damrned, now is the paper's cry
It's said to have a curse on put there in days gone by
By some old witch burnt on the Hill at least that's what we're told
To hear such things makes me feel ill now I am growing gold.
Coggeshall in my day knew nothing of all this
We were happy folks us yokels we led a life of bliss.
The village Bobby walked the streets he called each kid by name
There were hardly any *goings on* before the days of fame.
The 1980's was the start of all the shame and trouble
Murders, suicides and scandals, followed at the double
It seems a shame to see my town get bad news by the score
It happens to the new folk there, not to us ones of yours.
I feel sorry for my little town but suppose it's good for trade
People come to see the place and if it makes the grade.
Ah, Coggeshall in my time, I remember how things were
In my days of happy childhood when such things did not occur
It was known for being tranquil and I know that this is true
I only hope in future it takes on a better hue.
Coggeshall in my day, to live there was a pleasure
I'm not sure if it is today, but my memories I'll treasure.

Joan Hambly

The Once and the Now

A distinct fancy 'it started here!' is in the air,
Standing ovation for our White Sea Defence;
Hellfire throughout the war, a different land today.
A certain Churchill - he did visit here you know!
Those days are now gone; far away, together society relishes.

A castle of war, many face of leader and time,
Battles are plenty, the people remain ever strong:
'The face that denies despair heavily shed onto one.'

Recent times develop - a King in time a tourist,
Cairns the figurehead, in history he did his people proud.
The garden of England, its produce stands grand.

Its traditional people, allotments stripe with goodness,
Newspaper in the morning, everyday quite content,
A moan every now and then, refreshing the air,
Giving up that shall never do!

A force to attempt, trample their spirit,
The front-line men, women and children:
Determination never diminished!

The nineties, a look of *space-age confrontation*,
Tunnel, town affected, a meal on a ship is the key!
People, diversion to another,
Under mud, luxury to many extents:
Typical crossover, respect has remained.

The town in past, home to varied races,
Roman's felt at ease, straight roads; extravagance!
King's and Queen's took upon the corner of our country,
On the straights, not far out at sea;
The White is clearly seen, grass patches,
Here is home, the bluebirds fly over,
A welcoming sight, to warm ones heart.

Tony Watson

Canterbury Cathedral

Dominating
Triumphant,
All encompassing
Wearing Time's ravages
With dignified splendour.
Fingers probing the skyline
Green carpets,
Surrounding her base
Majestic.
Magnificent
Sanctuary from teeming pace.

Madeleine J Croll

Our Village

In the old days it was called the Treacle Mines!
Our lovely village that stands upon thick clay,
But our gardeners say it is great for the roses,
So who are we to say, 'nay?'

You ought to have been at our Village Fete,
Every sweet smelling flower you can name,
The veggies all new, crispy, coloured and polished!
Put most TV adverts to shame.

Two village greens and their cricket teams,
Keep our men contended for hours, with their scoring,
But the Beer Festival, down at the *pub* called *The Swan*,
In no time at all had them snoring!

There's more going on here than in the big town,
Community dinners, keep fit and come dancing!
Football in winter, socials and bingo,
Competitive tennis to keep them all prancing!

Do not tell everyone, but you'll see if you look,
That we have celebrities, they like living round here,
That handsome young man, with the big red book,
The political reporter, been so big through the years.

On bright snowy days, the kids get such a thrill,
They all go a-sledging, on Telegraph Hill.
We are mentioned you know in the Doomsday Book,
There's a plaque on the Green, come! Take a look!

We take pride in our shops, all along the Parade,
I know that sounds pompous, but it's all very proper,
Everyone's helpful, and their concern is repaid,
By both young and ancient, as well as the diligent shopper.

So if you are passing this way on some sunny day,
Take a rest on the Green, or down by the Fountain,
You will find that your problems have shrunk down
To Mole-Hills, instead of prodigious mountains!

F Mullis

Borough to Borough

My home, once Brighthelestone,
The sea its setting,
Gleams gold and blue
And silver too,
Bedazzling
My memory,
A haunt of childhood,
A mother's hand, and kisses,
A tapestry woven
Marvellously - to end
In dream texture
On the edge of sleep.
'How could you leave,'
I'm asked, 'to settle here,
Near Sutton, Surrey?'
'A whim' I cry, 'A move by chance'
Or did some higher power
That knew the ache in me
For verse, for study's calm,
For music, pen, research,
Call me hence,
South-Easterner,
No seascape near,
No hectic history,
To worship
Ever humbly
In a Borough Library -
No salt-sea breeze to cool
But the very air of
Peace?

Ruth Daviat

Wealden Clay

The summer twilight has slipped away,
The earth still warm from the heat of day,
The swallows swoop through the evening air
And night comes down like a blessing.

The badgers stir and the foxes bark
From Devil's Den out to Noah's Ark,
A darker gold clothes the fields of corn
As night-time weaves their dressing.

Out Beltring way, where the hops climb high,
The evening breeze breathes their lullaby
Past idle oasts down to home and farm,
And children sleep without fearing.

Though cider-presses stand silent now,
At Goudhurst fruit ripens on the bough,
For summer's older by one more day,
- And harvest home is nearing.

From Brasted Chart out to Edenbridge,
From Cowden Pound up to Bidborough Ridge,
From Hadlow Stair to the Chiding Stone,
The Weald of Kent lies sleeping.

Their father's bones may my children lay
In Wealden stone and in Wealden clay,
That where I loved when my heart was young
May hold me in its keeping.

Kit Griffiths

The Jewel in the Crown

The garden of England, it's always been,
Hops, corn and apples, strawberries and cream,
All that you need for a life that's content,
Is here to be had in glorious Kent.

Motorways, railways with Networker trains,
A young university bursting with brains,
There's ferry or tunnel if Europe's your bent,
They're first past the post in go-ahead Kent.

Dog and horse racing, culture and sports
Rural pursuits or seaside resorts,
Everything's here for your enjoyment,
You can really relax in leisurely Kent.

Oast houses, mansions, bungalows, farms,
Fisherman's cottages, stately tithe barns,
Castles, townhouses, houseboat, or tent,
You'll be at rest in homeloving Kent.

It's own native dialect soft on the ear
Wine for your table or thirst quenching beer,
Rivers and meadows, life's on the ascent,
You'll want for nothing in heavenly Kent.

From Thanet to Dartford or Canterbury,
Royal Wells, Maidstone, Hythe or Herne Bay
Wherever you go you'll be glad you were sent,
To wonderful, friendly, welcoming Kent.

Roger Wenham

Guildford Town

Come to Guildford Town
When you are in Surrey.
Linger for a while,
Don't be in a hurry.

See our ancient clock
And steeply cobbled street,
Something quite unique,
Not easy on the feet!

Seek the ruined castle,
It's mainly now the keep.
There, knights of old and
Mediaeval Maidens sleep.

Walk up to the Mount,
It lives up to its name!
Lewis Carrol's sleeping here,
His Alice books brought fame.

Laze upon the river bank,
Where longboats weave the Wey.
Doze, dream, and then decide
To come again one day.

Margaret Tunnell

Romney Marsh

The murmuring sea washes over the sand
Whispering stories of sea and land.
Of the land that once belonged to the sea,
Of its riches given up, reluctantly.
Now grasses wave and talk to the breeze
There are flowers, wild and pretty, hedgerows
And trees.
It is here you can feel at peace in the calm.
The quietness only broken by the call of birds
And the bleat of a lamb.
The quaint little churches and the villages that boast,
Of the smugglers run, straight in from the coast -
Long ago.
Swirling mist threads long fingers
Through the green of the marsh as there it lingers,
With ghostly stealth it cloaks to hide,
The landscape that disappears inside.
Romney Marsh shows its changing moods,
Hear the sound of the wind, rising high.
Storm clouds are massing in the sky.
Furious raindrops lash and sting
Filling the dykes to their very brim.
Sunrays then filter through the clean bright air
Bringing warmth and life to all that is bare.
I never want to leave the Romney Marsh.
Remote, serene, sometimes harsh.
With a quiet beauty, it is there
I would rather be than anywhere.

Pamela Dean

The Garden

Sight and sound and smell
Oh how my senses yell
I must add taste and touch
Aware there is so much.

Back garden, the old fashioned kind
I wonder what I will find
Plants, shrubs, bushes,
Grass, ivy, rushes.

An old tree stump
Lavender, lupines in a clump
Primroses climbing the wall
Roses growing so tall.

The lawn with some weeds
The birds fly down to feed
Buttercups, daisies, clover,
Of this garden I'm a lover.

Hanging baskets on the fence
The foledge is so dense
Of different shades and hues
I really cannot lose.

I've only lived here a few short weeks
It's like a game of hide and seek
Every day I find something new
Can this really be true?

My own little garden at last
But now the dye is cast
It got me in it's spell
The sights, the sounds, the smell.

Pauline Carroll

Memories

As I walk this downland turf again
And look out across the coastal plain,
The scent of honeysuckle mint and wild thyme,
Brings memories of journeys past flooding to my mind.

I've looked over fields of ripening corn,
Hedgerowed meadows where lambs are born,
Ribbons of water that thread their way,
Hurrying to meet the salt sea spray.

Walked in the dark shadows of ancient yew,
Through tall grass wet with dew.
Stood on the place they buried kings,
Where high above the skylark sings.

Windmills standing white and strong,
Reminder of a time long gone.
Steam engines that worked with untold power,
Heard church clocks mark the passing hour.

Watched strong shire horses pulling hard,
Wagons of hay to the farm rick yard.
I've heard the buzzards eerie cry,
On powerful wing he soars the sky.

When shadows lengthen and fading light,
Brings forth the creatures of the night.
Badgers and fox cubs play,
Welcoming the end of day.

I've travelled far, seen mountains bold,
Glaciers a thousand years old.
Rivers wide and chasms deep,
But these are the memories I keep.

Stephen Pratt

My Home County

The garden of England is my birthplace
The white cliffs, impressive cathedral towns and the Medway,
I'm a man of Kent and proud of it
Now we've got the channel tunnel coming our way.

Little trains, majestic castles, the world's busiest seaport
Hop farms with beautiful countryside to visit,
So like my grandparents I'm Dovorian born and bred
And if I had to leave I know I would miss it.

Susan Sherwood

Ancient and Modern

The village is bathed in morning mist,
The park has been kissed with dew.
Stark trees are clad in silvery bark
The paths are fresh and new.

But now from the depths of the river,
A hammering sound is heard.
Smoke rises from a ghostly furnace.
The bellows have been disturbed.

Trees turned to ash, the cinderheaps grew
The fleet need ammunition,
And *Strangers* worked once in our small town
Making the shot and cannon.

The smooth mill pond has images of
An outdated industry.
Updated buildings and waterwheels
Show recycled paper mills.

Our Liphook once has a Staging Post.
The traffic crossed in the square,
And from East to West - then North to South
All travellers rested there.

The motorcade, now wings its way by
On a modern carriageway.
But the traffic becalmed village square
Is not deserted and bare.

Still standing, the ancient Chestnut,
Hears an echo from the past.
'Think of the young folk and walk on down
Hampshire's historical paths.'

Barbara Battensby

The North Downs

I walked across the Downs today
The wind through my hair and the rain on my face.
I looked down upon the woods I love
And knew no man created this place.

I climbed upon the topmost mound
Oblivious of the wind and rain,
Heard the songbird high above
Saw the fields of growing grain
Gazed o'er the valley where earth meets sky
With concrete jungle in between
The desecration of the land -
Grey, amidst what once was green.

I've travelled to other counties
North, South, East and West,
Their woods and valleys I have seen
But the county I love best
Remains still this garden of England
Where much beauty still is found,
Framed - like a giant picture
Edged with green by these Downs.

I stood, with my thoughts in solitude,
The rain now beating on my face
And as I stood, 'twas then I knew!
I knew that God created this place.

V Garratt

Felpham Seafront

Among the T-shirted holidaymakers
He was conspicuous in jacket and tie,
Clutching black leather briefcase in one hand
Marks and Spencer bag in the other.
Fishermen hauled their boats ashore,
Leaving oozing tractor trails in the wet sand.
Tourists gawked at Blake's
Quaint thatched cottage,
Then clattered, chattering
Into the tea room. Children
Shrieked in the chill salt water.
He sat alone on the sea wall,
In his dark suit cocoon.
A beach ball bounced at his feet,
He kicked it back apologetically.
We went home for tea,
To make shell animals.

A black leather briefcase was found
On the tide-line the next morning.

Alison Batcock

Untitled

Although I've never liked the place,
I always return to it with a groan.
As at the end of the day what matters,
Is the fact I call it home.

I could travel the corners of the world.
And tell stories of where I went.
But I'll never actually appreciate,
Good old Ashford, Kent.

I've already been to some places,
That cover quite a range.
But the fact that's always amazed me,
Is that Ashfords never changed.

The town may alter cosmetically
But it's never really made a dent,
Or even the slightest impression,
On the back yard of County Kent.

Its never actually moved with the times
Its always taken it slow
So when the tunnel was announced
It was obviously a blow.

So for the sake of improvement
We decided to flatten what we had
But instead of getting any better,
We've gone from worst to bad

So now there's nothing for the locals
Or the foreigner that may drop in
They may as well shoot through to London
Because the town can't offer a thing.

A Cussens

If Only

Why were we given the eyes to see beauty, the mind
To appreciate beauty and the nose to smell scented
Flowers, but can only mar this beauty, slowly and surely,
Field by field, wood by wood? We are covering Kent with
Tacky houses and concrete roads.

If only we were like the lemming;
To Beachy Head we would go and into the sea would
Dive.
So that nature could have a little time to revive.

Michael J Hills

Rochester

A city of great expectations
That's what they say on the telly,
But mostly, it's just home to us
Mum, Dad, sisters Beth and Kellie.
Many parts of it have changed its true,
But still it keeps some old world charm,
And in the riverside gardens
Where folk stroll arm in arm
A castle stands, magnificently
In Norman times was built
And from our Saxon cathedral
Oft comes the sweetest lilt.
There's a festival of Dickens
It takes place in early June
And each day a big parade
Which starts just after noon -
Now this is really something
The costumes are no grand
Miss Havisham, Bill Sykes, all there,
Last, but not least, a band.
I shouldn't forget, in summer
A festival of art
Lots of things to see and do
Successful, from the start
A school, founded by Henry the Eighth
Some character was he,
I could tell you so much more
But, why don't you come and see
The city that is Rochester
So steeped, in history.

Wendy Cudd

St. Hilary's Eyes

On the crest of a windy brow through St. Hilary's eyes
Above a peopled assembly where only ghosts pry,
The plains of my early life wander down to the sea
Fostering films steeped in memories played back on a plea.

In my eyes lives a wooded hill where a forest once dwelt
In the bowels of its hidden caves smugglers would melt,
On the tor sits a windmill with its old battered sails
Which once beckoned proudly towards the mountains of Wales.

Etched on the playing fields on its long grassy shores
Dreams hatched from a somnolence which learning procures,
'Twas a school fighting gallantry in the name of St. George
Upholding all principals and dying by the sword.

Crawling past a sleepy lane 'tis a river which ghosts
Along side a factory's fumes where indulgency boasts,
You can taste every breath upon the thin chocolate breeze
Showering down incessantly upon the spring flavoured trees.

Ghosts prowl the castle walls capturing dreams in the air
Staring out to an empty sea are memories they share,
A lighthouse points proudly to the sky like a spear
Emanating upwards to where dreams disappear.

Brickwork's and hospitals and sandhills all went
Games played on the nerves of all neighbours repent,
Lives forged from the love of a childhood would drift
Away from the arms of a mothers one gift.

Just the memories are left once benevolence flees
All eaten by progress in time consumed seas,
On the crest of a windy brow a church muffles a sigh
Of my life fostering dreams through St Hilary's eyes.

David Bridgewater